The Poems and Hymns
of Christ's Sweet Singer

FRANCES RIDLEY HAVERGAL

*The Poems and Hymns
of Christ's Sweet Singer*

FRANCES RIDLEY HAVERGAL

SELECTED BY

Tacey Bly

KEATS PUBLISHING, INC.
New Canaan, Connecticut

The Poems and Hymns of Christ's Sweet Singer
Frances Ridley Havergal

ISBN: 0-87983-163-4 (hardbound)
       0-87983-164-2 (paperback)

Library of Congress Catalog Card: 77-865-49

Printed in the United States of America

Keats Publishing, Inc.
36 Grove Street, New Canaan, Connecticut 06840

Affectionately dedicated to
Mrs. Beryl White of "Serenity", Lowestoft, Suffolk, England, who has kept alive a flame of interest in Frances Ridley Havergal, which flame has become the brand that now lights other fires. All gracious thanks for her generosity in loaning us five old and precious books to make this book possible.

THE TWO PATHS

Via Dolorosa and Via Giojosa (Suggested by a picture)

MY Master, they have wronged Thee and Thy love!
They only told me I should find the path
A Via Dolorosa all the way!
Even Thy sweetest singers only sang
Of pressing onward through the same sharp thorns,
With bleeding footsteps, through the chill dark mist,
Following and struggling till they reach the light,
The rest, the sunshine of the far beyond.
The anthems of the pilgrimage were set
In most pathetic minors, exquisite,
Yet breathing sadness more than any praise.
Thy minstrels let the fitful breezes make
Aeolian moans on their entrusted harps,
Until the listeners thought that this was all
The music Thou hadst given. And so the steps
That halted where the two ways met and crossed,
The broad and narrow, turned aside in fear,
Thinking the radiance of their youth must pass
In sombre shadows if they followed Thee:
Hearing afar such echoes of one strain,
The cross, the tribulation, and the toil.
The conflict, and the clinging in the dark.
What wonder that the dancing feet are stayed
From entering the only path of peace!
Master, forgive them! Tune their harps anew,
And put a new song in their mouths for Thee,
And make Thy chosen people joyful in Thy love.

UNDER HIS SHADOW

CONTENTS

The Poems and Hymns
of Christ's Sweet Singer

FRANCES RIDLEY HAVERGAL

FRANCES RIDLEY HAVERGAL
(1836-1879)

Frances Ridley Havergal was the daughter of Jane and William Henry Havergal, then Rector of Astley in Worcestershire. Her middle name, which she was always proud to use, was in honor of her godfather, Reverend W. H. Ridley, Rector of Hambleden. This distinguished clergyman was descended from Bishop Ridley, who was martyred with Latimer. Frances was the youngest of a family of six children, and unquestionably the beloved pet. Her sisters and brothers were, from oldest to youngest, Jane Miriam, Henry, Maria, Ellen and Francis (Frank).

The family was apparently quite a happy one. Maria reminisces in *Memorials* about their Sunday evening hymn singing, picturing young Frances sitting on her father's lap, "a very fairy with her golden curls." She recalls the pervading Christian atmosphere of their home: "Our parents' prayers and example in searching the Scriptures, and their loving cheery ways, activity and punctuality, were the keynotes of our child-life." Some simple, pure and delightfully sweet spirit of this upbringing is captured — almost as if by accident — in a poem written by this popular inspirational poet when she was seven years old.

> Sunday is a pleasant day,
> When we to church do go;
> For there we sing and read and pray,
> And hear the sermon too.
>
> On Sunday hear the village bells;
> It seems as if they said,
> Go to the church where the pastor tells
> How Christ for men has bled.

And if we love to pray and read
While we are in our youth,
The Lord will help us in our need
And keep us in His truth.

When Frances was nine years old, her family began the first of a series of moves from one ministry to another. At this time they went to St. Nicholas Rectory in Worcestershire. It was much less rural than Astley, and the little girl pined for the countryside in her rare moments of melancholy.

She was an extremely intelligent and sensitive child. Nor did she lack spunk. Called "Little Quicksilver" by her father, she easily lived up to the nickname with her bright, lively disposition. First taught by her sister Miriam, Frances could read easy books at the age of three; at four she could read the Bible and write roundhand. She was precocious in spiritual matters as well. According to her own recollections, she hadn't a thought of God until she was six years old. Then began the "longing to be a Christian" which caused her to lie awake at night praying for faith, or trying to think of nothing but God. She also recollected reading the Bible fervently, determined to find the Eternal Life it promised to a child of God. She did have sensibility of herself as a sinner, and knew in her mind that God had provided for her salvation, but it would take some more time for this truth to take root in the heart.

Jane Havergal, Frances's mother, died in June of 1848 after a long, wasting illness. Looking back, Miss Havergal says in *Memorials* that this suffering and dying should have made a great impression on her — but that in fact, the exuberant twelve-year-old was not weighed down by the loss, or by much of anything. Yet we know from some of her other writings that Frances's mother's last words to her affected her deeply: "Fanny dear, pray to God to prepare you for all that He is preparing for you." This did become her life's prayer.

As was the custom, Frances was sent to Belmont, a boarding school for girls when she was thirteen. Mrs. Teed, the principal, finishing up her last year of administration, prayed that she would be blessed in leading many girls to Christ that last year. Some of Frances's friends did become Christians; Frances could not. What she felt was, above all else, confusion and anguish.

One by one, her best friends were converted there, at school. Her own call finally came during a vacation visit to her sister Miriam in 1851. Caroline Cook, the woman who would shortly become Reverend Havergal's second wife, helped fifteen-year-old Frances put her trust in Christ. At the time of her conversion she realized that what she had given to Christ, He would be well able to *keep*. This revelation became a special characteristic of her faith, and part of her own unique message to fellow Christians. The Lord's ability to preserve His faithful is the theme particularly exemplified in *Kept for the Master's Use*, the last book written by Frances Ridley Havergal.

The next year her studies were interrupted by erysipelas, a skin disesase on her face and head. The forced inactivity imposed frustration and disappointment on "Little Quicksilver." But in 1853, her father's problems with cataracts initiated a change of scene. They went to Germany to consult medical experts. Frances, recovered from erysipelas, was allowed to enroll in a public school in Dusseldorf. Not one of the girls she encountered there was concerned in the least about God. This brought out the fighting spirit, and a one-girl campaign to work and win souls for the Lord. The campaign may not have had an ostensible effect on her companions, but it certainly did strengthen Frances's own young walk with Jesus.

The end of this school year brought an end to all formal studies. At seventeen, the dedicated young woman was prepared to take on adult responsibilities, sharing in the management of family life. However, these duties did not exclude study, and Frances continued on her own to concentrate particularly on languages, eventually achieving proficiency in Italian, French, German, Latin, Greek and Hebrew.

Back in England at St. Nicholas Rectory in 1854, she continued writing poetry as she had done since she was seven, and won several prizes. One competition awarded her six books. Characteristically, she kept one and sold the others for a contribution to missionary work.

At this time, Elizabeth Clay, a schoolgirl friend and also a devoted Christian, became Frances's constant companion. The two young women began systematically to learn the Scriptures, and in time, Frances knew all the Gospels, Epistles, Revelation, the Psalms and Isaiah; later she added the minor prophets. She also began what was to become a lifelong mission — the teaching of children in Sunday school. The very model of a perfect teacher, she kept meticulous records, following through the development of each child's religious learning and experience. Anyone familiar with her poetry might observe her shining rapport with the spirit of children (her own childlike spirit evident in the wonder and freshness in her verse); her joyous hymns still ring out in Sunday schools all over the world.

Reverend Havergal's health continued to decline, and as a result, the family moved again in 1860 to a quieter, less demanding rectory in the country. The year after that Frances went to live with her brother Henry's family at Oakhampton, where she tutored her two nieces. She enjoyed the task enormously, and the change undoubtedly improved her own frail health. The children (and perhaps their parents) conspired to keep Frances from indulging so intensely in her studies; she could not avoid diversion even if she wanted to. Nevertheless, during her stay at Oakhampton she became a regular contributor of hymns (to which her father most often composed the music) and poems to *Good Words* and other Christian magazines.

She also became a popular soloist at the Philharmonic Society. According to letters quoted by her sister in *Memorials*, Miss Havergal was gifted with a truly lovely voice and fine choral ability. Music must have been her next love after God. Handel's music particularly delighted her, and she used it and that of other great composers to carry the Gospel message into many homes and social gatherings, to many audiences. In a free and creative spirit she also composed some music of her own while living with her brother's family.

Actually, much of Frances Ridley Havergal's verses were composed in a free and creative spirit — or at least they were an inspired and spontaneous reaction to the people and circumstances around her, rather than the results of an academic effort. In two different anecdotes we get a glimpse of her facile composing ability. In *Memorials* we read: "When visiting Perry Barr she walked to the boy's schoolroom, and being very tired, she leaned against the playground wall while Mr. Snepp (editor of the *Songs of Grace and Glory*, 1822) went in. Returning in ten minutes, he found her scribbling on an envelope, and at his request she handed him the hymn just penciled." This hymn was the very famous "Golden Harps Are Sounding."

Also from *Memorials* we learn that Miss Havergal went to stay at a friend's house in February, 1874, just a scant month after she had taken a further, most profound step in her own commitment to Christ. There were about ten other guests staying with this family; some were not Christians, some professed to be Christians, but to a discerning eye, not very happy ones. She longed and prayed that all of these friends might come to know the joy and peace that she was experiencing — one can imagine the exuberance of her witness and the earnestness of her prayers, which were answered! A new spiritual life did indeed begin for these people, and on the last night of her visit, Frances Havergal was too excited to sleep. She stayed awake and wrote another of her most cherished hymns, "Take My Life and Let It Be."

In the following years, the cross of bodily pain accompanied steadily deteriorating health, and to bear it, this saintly woman often turned to Jesus for help. The darker notes in her poetry can be traced to this particular trial. Committed as she was, and a member of the body of Christ, she was not immune from the trials of the flesh, nor of the human spirit. Like anyone else, she too was plagued from time to time by doubts and impatience. She too struggled to "endure." Her sister quotes her in *Memorials:*

> I had hoped that a kind of table-land had been
> reached in my journey, where I might walk awhile
> in the light, without the weary succession of rock and
> hollow, crag and morass, stumbling and striving; but
> I seem borne back into all the old difficulties of the
> way, with many sin-made aggravations. I think the
> great root of all my troubles and aggravations is
> that I do not now make an unreserved surrender of
> myself to God; and until this is done I shall know
> no peace.

In 1867, Frances settled at Leamington with Mrs. Havergal and her father, who was now retired. After his death in 1870, his daughter undertook the editing of his *Havergal's Psalm-*

ody. This book followed his *A Hundred Psalm and Hymn Tunes* (1859), as well as other books about hymns. Frances's own hymn-writing career was already under way, for *The Ministry of Song* had been published in 1868.

The campaign begun at school in Dusseldorf was never forsaken. No matter what her condition, or what else she did, a prime concern was always to bring the light of the Gospel to *everyone* with whom Frances Havergal came in contact, whether it was the girl in the local laundry or the waitress in a hotel in Switzerland. Throughout her life she continued to devote her skill and time to teaching music, leading prayer groups, and other such work at various societies, including the Y.W.C.A., in which she always remained an active member.

In 1872 the work began on *Under the Surface,* a book of poems which was published two years later. But periodic bouts of illness prevented many plans for writing from being accomplished: her captivity must have been a severe burden for such a creative, constantly productive person.

About this time an unidentified friend sent a little book called "All for Jesus." Perhaps it came just at the right moment to encourage her; at any rate, it deeply touched her spirit, and as her sister says, "the 'sunken ravines' were now forever passed." The hope that some kind of basic unshakeable peace could be attained was apparently realized.

External circumstances were certainly not conducive to peace and contentment. In 1874, Frances suffered with fever, dull and persistent headaches and she grew increasingly ill. It seems to have been typhoid fever. In the year 1875 she came close to death. She survived this, and between periods of sickness and physical collapse went out singing, lecturing, evangelizing and working for Christ. She made a final trip to her beloved Switzerland with her sister Maria; once more she caught a serious cold and remained in bed for a month, delaying the journey home. Home, at the end of her life, was in Wales, where Frances and Maria shared a house. Here a vigorous correspondence was kept up, *Kept for the Master's Use, Starlight Through the Shadows,* and *Morning Stars* were all prepared for publication, and plans made for a trip to Ireland. But after a Gospel Temperance meeting held outdoors during a treacherous afternoon in May, 1879, Miss Havergal caught one of the colds that plagued her during a lifelong susceptibility, and this time she did not recover. She was forty-two years old when she died. Some of her last words betray her confidence and joy in Christ: "It's home the faster." . . . "Splendid to be so near the gate of Heaven." . . . "So beautiful to go."

She was buried at Astley Rectory. Her tombstone is engraved as she had requested: "The blood of Jesus Christ His Son cleanseth us from all sin."

Frances Ridley Havergal is becoming a legend. Except for *Kept for the Master's Use*, her books are out of print. Her partial autobiography and collection of letters, diaries and commentary by her sister *(Memorials)* is a lovely old volume — also out of print — in theological libraries. Even her name seems to be increasingly less well-known — ironically — as her hymns are engraved deeper into our hearts and traditions with each passing year. Perhaps this book will serve to remind us of the very real woman, and her very real spiritual struggles that lie just "under the surface" of the familiar words we sing habitually and even sometimes absentmindedly.

CONSECRATION

If a man therefore purge himself

from these [sin], he shall

be a vessel unto honour,

sanctified and meet for

the master's use, and prepared

unto every good work. II TIMOTHY 2:21

CONSECRATION HYMN

Here we offer and present unto
Thee, O Lord, ourselves, our souls
and bodies, to be a reasonable,
holy, and lively sacrifice unto Thee.
Book of Common Prayer

TAKE my life, and let it be
Consecrated, Lord, to Thee.

Take my moments and my days;
Let them flow in ceaseless praise.

Take my hands, and let them move
At the impulse of Thy love.

Take my feet, and let them be
Swift and "beautiful" for Thee.

Take my voice, and let me sing
Always, only, for my King.

Take my lips, and let them be
Filled with messages from Thee.

Take my silver and my gold;
Not a mite would I withhold.

Take my intellect, and use
Every power as Thou shalt choose.

Take my will, and make it Thine;
It shall be no longer mine.

Take my heart, it *is* Thine own;
It shall be Thy royal throne.

Take my love; my Lord, I pour
At Thy feet its treasure-store.

Take myself, and I will be
Ever, *only*, ALL for Thee.

LOYAL RESPONSES

TRUE-HEARTED, WHOLE-HEARTED

TRUE-HEARTED, whole-hearted, faithful and loyal,
 King of our lives, by Thy grace we will be!
Under Thy standard, exalted and royal,
 Strong in Thy strength, we will battle for Thee!

True-hearted, whole-hearted! Fullest allegiance
 Yielding henceforth to our glorious King;
Valiant endeavour and loving obedience
 Freely and joyously now would we bring.

True-hearted! Saviour, Thou knowest our story;
 Weak are the hearts that we lay at Thy feet,
Sinful and treacherous! yet, for Thy glory,
 Heal them, and cleanse them from sin and deceit.

Whole-hearted! Saviour, beloved and glorious,
 Take Thy great power, and reign Thou alone,
Over our wills and affections victorious,
 Freely surrendered, and wholly Thine own.

Half-hearted, *false*-hearted! Heed we the warning!
 Only the whole can be perfectly true;
Bring the whole offering, all timid thought scorning,
 True-hearted only if whole-hearted too.

Half-hearted! Saviour, shall aught be withholden,
 Giving Thee part who hast given us all?

Blessings outpouring, and promises golden
  Pledging, with never reserve or recall.

Half-hearted! Master, shall any who know Thee
  Grudge Thee their lives, who hast laid down Thine own?
Nay; we would offer the hearts that we owe Thee —
  Live for Thy love and Thy glory alone.

Sisters, dear sisters, the call is resounding,
  Will ye not echo the silver refrain,
Mighty and sweet, and in gladness abounding, —
  "True-hearted, whole-hearted!" ringing again?

Jesus is with us, His rest is before us,
  Brightly His standard is waving above.
Brothers, dear brothers, in gathering chorus,
  Peal out the watchword of courage and love!

Peal out the watchword, and silence it never,
  Song of our spirits, rejoicing and free!
"True-hearted, whole-hearted, now and for ever,
  King of our lives, by Thy grace we will be."

LOYAL RESPONSES

SET APART

*Know that the Lord hath set
apart him that is godly for
Himself.* Psalm 4:3

SET apart for Jesus!
Is not this enough,
Though the desert prospect
Open wild and rough?
Set apart for His delight,
Chosen for His holy pleasure,
Sealed to be His special treasure!
Could we choose a nobler joy? — and would we if we might?

Set apart to serve Him,
Ministers of light,
Standing in His presence,
Ready day or night!
Chosen for His service blest,
He would have us always willing
Like the angel-hosts fulfilling
Swiftly and rejoicingly, each recognized behest.

Set apart to praise Him,
Set apart for this!
Have the blessed angels
Any truer bliss?
Soft the prelude, though so clear;
Isolated tones are trembling;
But the chosen choir, assembling,
Soon shall sing together, while the universe shall hear.

Set apart to love Him,
And His love to know!
Not to waste affection
On a passing show.
Called to give Him life and heart,
Called to pour the hidden treasure,
That none other claims to measure,
Into His beloved hand! thrice-blessed "set apart!"

Set apart for ever
For Himself alone!
Now we see our calling
Gloriously shown!
Owning, with no secret dread,
This our holy separation,
Now the crown of consecration
Of the Lord our God shall rest upon our willing head![1]

LOYAL RESPONSES

[1] Numbers 6:7

HE IS THY LIFE

JESUS, Thy life is mine!
Dwell evermore in me;
    And let me see
That nothing can untwine
    My life from Thine.

Thy life in me be shown!
Lord, I would henceforth seek
    To think and speak
Thy thoughts, Thy words alone,
    No more my own.

Thy love, Thy joy, Thy peace,
Continuously impart
    Unto my heart;
Fresh springs, that never cease,
    But still increase.

Thy blest reality
Of resurrection power,
    Thy Church's dower,
Life more abundantly,
    Lord give to me!

Thy fullest gift, O Lord,
Now at Thy feet I claim,
    Through Thy dear name!
And touch the rapturous chord
    Of praise forth poured.

Jesus, my life is Thine,
And evermore shall be
Hidden in Thee!
For nothing can untwine
Thy life from mine.

LOYAL RESPONSES

WHAT THOU WILT

DO what Thou wilt! Yes, only do
    What seemeth good to Thee:
Thou art so loving, wise, and true,
    It must be best for me.

Send what Thou wilt; or beating shower,
    Soft dew, or brilliant sun;
Alike in still or stormy hour,
    My Lord, Thy will be done.

Teach what Thou wilt; and make me learn
    Each lesson full and sweet,
And deeper things of God discern
    While sitting at Thy feet.

Say what Thou wilt; and let each word
    My quick obedience win;
Let loyalty and love be stirred
    To deeper glow within.

Give what Thou wilt; for then I know
    I shall be rich indeed;
My King rejoices to bestow
    Supply for every need.

Take what Thou wilt, beloved Lord,
    For I have all in Thee!
My own exceeding great reward,
    Thou, Thou Thyself shalt be!

CLOSING CHORDS

THE FULLNESS OF GOD

TAKE us, Lord, oh take us truly,
  Mind and soul and heart and will;
Empty us and cleanse us thoroughly,
  Then with all Thy fulness fill.

Lord, we ask it, hardly knowing
  What this wondrous gift may be;
But fulfill to overflowing, —
  Thy great meaning let us see.

Make us in Thy royal palace
  Vessels worthy for the King;
From Thy fulness fill our chalice,
  From Thy never-failing spring.

Father, by this blessed filling,
  Dwell Thyself in us, we pray;
We are waiting, Thou art willing,
  Fill us with Thyself today!

THREEFOLD PRAISE

NOT YOUR OWN

"NOT your own!" but His ye are,
　　Who hath paid a price untold
For your life, exceeding far
　　All earth's store of gems and gold.
With the precious blood of Christ,
Ransom treasure all unpriced,
Full redemption is procured,
Full salvation is assured.

"Not your own!" but His by right,
　　His peculiar treasure now,
Fair and precious in His sight,
　　Purchased jewels for His brow.
He will keep what thus He sought,
Safely guard the dearly bought,
Cherish that which He did choose,
Always love and never lose.

"Not your own!" but His, the King
　　His, the Lord of earth and sky —
His, to whom archangels bring
　　Homage deep and praises high.
What can royal birth bestow?
Or the proudest titles show?
Can such dignity be known
As the glorious name, "His own!"

"Not your own!" to Him ye owe
　　All your life and all your love;

Live, that ye His praise may show,
    Who is yet all praise above.
Every day and every hour,
Every gift and every power,
Consecrate to Him alone,
Who hath claimed you for His own.

Teach us Master, how to give
    All we have and are to Thee;
Grant us, Saviour, while we live,
    Wholly, only, Thine to be,
Henceforth be our calling high,
Thee to serve and glorify;
Ours no longer, but Thine own,
Thine for ever, Thine alone!

THE MINISTRY OF SONG

WHOSE I AM

JESUS, Master, whose I am,
    Purchased Thine alone to be,
By Thy blood, O spotless Lamb,
    Shed so willingly for me;
Let my heart be all Thine own,
Let me live to Thee alone.

Other lords have long held sway;
    Now, Thy name alone to bear,
Thy dear voice alone obey,
    Is my daily, hourly prayer.
Whom have I in heaven but Thee?
Nothing else my joy can be.

Jesus, Master! I am Thine;
    Keep me faithful, keep me near;
Let Thy presence in me shine
    All my homeward way to cheer.
Jesus! at Thy feet I fall,
Oh, be Thou my All-in-all.

THE MINISTRY OF SONG

CHRIST'S RECALL

RETURN!
   O wanderer from my side!
Soon droops each blossom of the darkening wild,
Soon melts each meteor which thy steps beguiled,
Soon is the cistern dry which thou hast hewn,
And thou wilt weep in bitterness full soon.
Return! ere gathering night shall shroud the way
Thy footsteps yet may tread, in this accepted day.

      Return!
   O erring, yet beloved!
I wait to bind thy bleeding feet, for keen
And rankling are the thorns where thou hast been;
I wait to give thee pardon, love, and rest;
Is not My joy to see thee safe and blest?
Return! I wait to hear once more thy voice,
To welcome thee anew, and bid thy heart rejoice.

      Return!
   O fallen, yet not lost!
Canst thou forget the Life for thee laid down,
The taunts, the scourging, and the thorny crown?
When o'er thee first My spotless robe I spread,
And poured the oil of joy upon thy head,
How did thy wakening heart within thee burn!
Canst thou remember all, and wilt thou not return?

      Return!
   O chosen of My love!
Fear not to meet thy beckoning Saviour's view,

Long ere I called thee by thy name, I knew
That very treacherously thou wouldst deal;
Now I have seen thy ways, yet I will heal.
Return! Wilt thou yet linger far from Me?
My wrath is turned away, I have redeemed thee.

THE MINISTRY OF SONG

"THE THINGS WHICH ARE BEHIND"

LEAVE behind earth's empty pleasure,
    Fleeting hope and changeful love;
Leave its soon-corroding treasure:
    There are better things above.

Leave, oh, leave thy fond aspirings,
    Bid thy restless heart be still;
Cease, oh, cease thy vain desirings,
    Only seek thy Father's will.

Leave behind thy faithless sorrow,
    And thine every anxious care;
He who only knows the morrow
    Can for thee its burden bear.

Leave behind the doubting spirit,
    And thy crushing load of sin;
Be thy mighty Saviour's merit,
    Life eternal thou shalt win.

Leave the darkness gathering o'er thee,
    Leave the shadow-land behind;
Realms of glory lie before thee;
    Enter in, and welcome find.

THE MINISTRY OF SONG

TO THEE

Lord, to whom shall we go?
John 6:68

I bring my sins to Thee,
    The sins I cannot count,
That all may cleansed be
    In Thy once opened Fount.
I bring them, Saviour, all to Thee,
The burden is too great for me.

My heart to Thee I bring,
    The heart I cannot read;
A faithless, wandering thing,
    An evil heart indeed.
I bring it, Saviour, now to Thee,
That fixed and faithful it may be.

To thee I bring my care,
    The care I cannot flee;
Thou wilt not only share,
    But bear it all for me.
O loving Saviour, now to Thee
I bring the load that wearies me.

I bring my grief to Thee,
    The grief I cannot tell;
No words shall needed be,
    Thou knowest all so well.
I bring the sorrow laid on me,
O suffering Saviour, now to Thee.

My joys to Thee I bring,
    The joys Thy love hath given,
That each may be a wing
    To lift me nearer heaven.
I bring them, Saviour, all to Thee,
For Thou hast purchased all for me.

My life I bring to Thee,
    I would not be my own;
O Saviour, let me be
    Thine ever, Thine alone.
My heart, my life, my all I bring
To Thee, my Saviour and my King!

UNDER THE SURFACE

"JESUS ONLY"

Matthew 17:8

"JESUS only!" In the shadow
　　Of the cloud so chill and dim,
We are clinging, loving, trusting,
　　He with us, and we with Him;
All unseen, though ever nigh,
"Jesus only" — all our cry.

"Jesus only!" In the glory,
　　When the shadows all are flown
Seeing Him in all His beauty,
　　Satisfied with Him alone;
May we join His ransomed throng,
"Jesus only" — all our song!

UNDER THE SURFACE

DEDICATION
OF WORK
AND TALENTS

*Commit thy works unto the Lord,
and thy thoughts shall be
established.* PROVERBS 16:3

LIFE MOSAIC

MASTER, to do great work for Thee, my hand
 Is far too weak! Thou givest what may suit —
 Some little chips to cut with care minute,
Or tint, or grave, or polish. Others stand
Before their quarried marble fair and grand,
 And make a life-work of the great design
 Which Thou hast traced; or, many-skilled, combine
To build vast temples, gloriously planned.
Yet take the tiny stones which I have wrought,
 Just one by one, as they were given by Thee,
Not knowing what came next in Thy wise thought.
Set each stone by Thy master-hand of grace,
 Form the mosaic as Thou wilt for me,
And in Thy temple-pavement give it place.

LIFE MOSAIC

WHOM I SERVE

JESUS, Master, whom I serve,
　　Though so feebly and so ill,
Strengthen hand and heart and nerve
　　All Thy bidding to fulfil;
Open Thou mine eyes to see
All the work Thou hast for me.

Lord, Thou needest not, I know,
　　Service such as I can bring;
Yet I long to prove and show
　　Full allegiance to my King.
Thou an honour art to me,
Let me be a praise to Thee.

Jesus, Master! wilt Thou use
　　One who owes Thee more than all?
As Thou wilt! I would not choose,
　　Only let me hear Thy call.
Jesus! let me always be
In Thy service glad and free.

THREEFOLD PRAISE

THE MINISTRY OF SONG

IN God's great field of labour
    All work is not the same;
He hath a service for each one
    Who loves His holy name.
And you, to whom the secrets
    Of all sweet sounds are known,
Rise up! for He hath called you
    To a mission of your own.
And, rightly to fulfill it,
    His grace can make you strong,
Who to your change hath given
    The Ministry of Song.

Sing to the little children,
    And they will listen well;
Sing grand and holy music,
    For they can feel its spell.
Tell them the tale of Jephthah;
    Then sing them what he said, —
"Deeper and deeper still," and watch
    How the little cheek grows red,
And the little breath comes quicker:
    They will ne'er forget the tale,
Which the song has fastened surely,
    As with a golden nail.

I remember, late one evening,
    How the music stopped; for hark!
Charlie's nursery door was open,

He was calling in the dark, —
"Oh no! I am not frightened,
    And I do not want a light;
But I cannot sleep for thinking
    Of the song you sang last night.
Something about a 'valley,'
    And 'make rough places plain,'
And 'Comfort ye;' so beautiful!
    Oh, sing it me again!"

Sing at the cottage bedside;
    They have no music there,
And the voice of praise is silent
    After the voice of prayer.
Sing of the gentle Saviour
    In the simplest hymns you know,
And the pain-dimmed eye will brighten
    As the soothing verses flow.
Better than loudest plaudits
    The murmured thanks of such,
For the King will stoop to crown them
    With His gracious "Inasmuch."

Sing, where the full-toned organ
    Resounds through aisle and nave,
And the choral praise ascendeth
    In concord sweet and grave.
Sing, where the village voices
    Fall harshly on your ear;
And, while more earnestly you join,
    Less discord you will hear.
The noblest and the humblest
    Alike are "common praise,"
And not for human ear alone
    The psalm and hymn we raise.

Sing in the deepening twilight,
    When the shadow of eve is nigh,
And her purple and golden pinions
    Fold o'er the western sky.

Sing in the silver silence,
 While the first moonbeams fall;
So shall your power be greater
 Over the hearts of all.
Sing till you bear them with you
 Into a holy calm,
And the sacred tones have scattered
 Manna, and myrrh, and balm.

Sing! that your song may gladden;
 Sing like the happy rills,
Leaping in sparkling blessing
 Fresh from the breezy hills.
Sing! that your song may silence
 The folly and the jest,
And the "idle word" be banished
 As an unwelcome guest.
Sing! that your song may echo,
 After the strain is past,
A link of the love-wrought cable
 That holds some vessel fast.

Sing to the tired and anxious;
 It is yours to fling a ray,
Passing indeed, but cheering,
 Across the rugged way.
Sing to God's holy servants,
 Weary with loving toil,
Spent with their faithful labour
 On oft ungrateful soil.
The chalice of your music
 All reverently bear,
For with the blessed angels
 Such ministry you share.

Sing when His mighty mercies
 And marvellous love you feel,
And the deep joy of gratitude
 Springs freshly as you kneel;
When words, like morning starlight,

Melt powerless, rise and sing!
And bring your sweetest music
  To Him, your gracious King.
Pour out your song before Him
  To whom our best is due;
Remember, He who hears your prayer
  Will hear your praises too.

Sing on in grateful gladness!
  Rejoice in this good thing
Which the Lord thy God hath given thee,
  The happy power to sing.
But yield to Him, the Sovereign,
  To whom all gifts belong,
In fullest consecration,
  Your Ministry of Song,
Until His mercy grant you
  That resurrection voice,
Whose only ministry shall be
  To praise Him and rejoice.

THE MINISTRY OF SONG

[38]

HAVE YOU NOT A WORD FOR JESUS?

O Lord, open Thou my lips; and my mouth
shall show forth Thy praise. Psalm 51:15

HAVE you not a word for Jesus? not a word to say for Him?
He is listening through the chorus of the burning seraphim!
HE IS LISTENING; does He hear you speaking of the things of earth,
Only of its passing pleasure, selfish sorrow, empty mirth?
He has spoken words of blessing, pardon, peace, and love to you,
Glorious hopes and gracious comfort, strong and tender, sweet and
       true:
Does He hear you telling others something of His love untold,
Overflowings of thanksgiving for His mercies manifold?

Have you not a word for Jesus? Will the world His praise proclaim?
Who shall speak if ye are silent? ye who know and love His name.
You, whom He hath called and chosen His own witnesses to be,
Will you tell your gracious Master, "Lord, we cannot speak
       for Thee"?
"Cannot!" though He suffered for you, died because He loved you
       so!
"Cannot!" though He has forgiven, making scarlet white as snow!
"Cannot!" though His grace abounding is your freely promised aid!
"Cannot!" though He stands beside you, though He says, "Be not
       afraid!"

Have you not a word for Jesus? Some, perchance, while ye are dumb,
Wait and weary for your message, hoping you will bid them
       "come;"
Never telling hidden sorrows, lingering just outside the door,
Longing for your hand to lead them into rest for evermore.
Yours may be the joy and honour His redeemed ones to bring,
Jewels for the coronation of your coming Lord and King.

Will you cast away the gladness thus your Master's joy to share,
All because a word for Jesus seems too much for you to dare?

What shall be our word for Jesus? Master, give it day by day;
Ever as the need arises, teach Thy children what to say.
Give us holy love and patience; grant us deep humility,
That of self we may be emptied, and our hearts be full of Thee;
Give us zeal and faith and fervour, make us winning, make us wise,
Single-hearted, strong, and fearless, — Thou hast called us, we will
    rise!
Let the might of Thy good Spirit go with every loving word;
And by hearts prepared and opened be our message always heard!

Yes, we have a word for Jesus! Living echoes we will be
Of Thine own sweet words of blessing, of Thy gracious "Come to
    Me."
Jesus, Master! yes, we love Thee, and, to prove our love would lay
Fruit of lips which Thou wilt open at Thy blessed feet today.
Many an effort it may cost us, many a heartbeat, many a fear,
But Thou knowest, and wilt strengthen, and Thy help is always
    near.
Give us grace to follow fully, vanquishing our faithless shame,
Feebly it may be, but truly, witnessing for Thy dear Name.

Yes, we have a word for Jesus! we will bravely speak for Thee,
And Thy bold and faithful soldiers, Saviour, we would henceforth
    be;
In Thy name set up our banners, while Thine own shall wave above,
With Thy crimson Name of Mercy, and Thy golden Name of Love,
Help us lovingly to labour, looking for Thy present smile,
Looking for Thy promised blessing, through the brightening "little
    while."
Words for Thee in weakness spoken, Thou wilt here accept and
    own,
And confess them in Thy glory, when we see Thee on Thy throne.

UNDER THE SURFACE

A WORKER'S PRAYER

LORD, speak to me, that I may speak
    In living echoes of Thy tone;
As Thou hast sought, so let me seek
    Thy erring children, lost and lone.

O lead me, Lord, that I may lead
    The wandering and the wavering feet;
O feed me, Lord, that I may feed
    Thy hungering ones with manna sweet.

O strengthen me, that while I stand
    Firm on the Rock and strong in Thee,
I may stretch out a loving hand
    To wrestlers with the troubled sea.

O teach me, Lord, that I may teach
    The precious things Thou dost impart;
And wing my words, that they may reach
    The hidden depths of many a heart.

O give Thine own sweet rest to me,
    That I may speak with soothing power
A word in Season, as from Thee,
    To weary ones in needful hour.

O fill me with Thy fulness, Lord,
    Until my very heart o'erflow

In kindling thought and glowing word,
    Thy love to tell, Thy praise to show.

O use me, Lord, use even me,
    Just as Thou wilt, and when, and where;
Until Thy blessed Face I see,
    Thy rest, Thy joy, Thy glory share.

UNDER THE SURFACE

CALLED

Partakers of the heavenly calling.
Hebrews 3:1

HOLY brethren, called and chosen by the sovereign Voice of Might,
See your high and holy calling out of darkness into light!
Called according to His purpose and the riches of His love;
Won to listen by the leading of the gentle heavenly Dove!

Called to suffer with our Master, patiently to run His race;
Called a blessing to inherit, called to holiness and grace;
Called to fellowship with Jesus by the Ever-Faithful One;
Called to His eternal glory, to the kingdom of His son.

Whom He calleth He preserveth, and His glory they shall see;
He is faithful that hath called you — He will do it, fear not ye!
Therefore, holy brethren, onward! thus ye make your calling sure;
For the prize of this high calling, bravely to the end endure.

UNDER THE SURFACE

CHURCH MISSIONARY JUBILEE HYMN

He shall see of the travail
of his soul, and shall be
satisfied.   Isaiah 53:11

REJOICE, with Jesus Christ today,
All ye who love His holy sway!
The travail of His soul is past,
He shall be satisfied at last.
Rejoice with Him, rejoice indeed,
For He shall see His chosen seed!
But ours the trust, the grand employ,
To work out this divinest joy.
Of all His own He loseth none,
They shall be gathered one by one;
He gathereth the smallest grain,
His travail shall not be in vain.
Arise and work! arise and pray
That He would haste the dawning day!
And let the silver trumpet sound,
Whenever Satan's slaves are found.
The vanquished foe shall soon be stilled,
The conquering Saviour's joy fulfilled,
Fulfilled in us, fulfilled in them,
His crown, His royal diadem.
Soon, soon our waiting eyes shall see
The Saviour's mighty Jubilee!
His harvest-joy is filling fast,
He shall be satisfied at last!

MISCELLANEOUS

ON THE LORD'S SIDE

Thine are we, David,
and on thy side,
thou son of Jesse.
I Chronicles 12:18

WHO is on the Lord's side?
  Who will serve the King?
Who will be His helpers,
  Other lives to bring?
Who will leave the world's side?
  Who will face the foe?
Who is on the Lord's side?
  Who for Him will go?
Response. By Thy call of mercy,
        By Thy grace divine,
      We are on the Lord's side;
        Saviour, we are Thine.

Not for weight of glory,
  Not for crown and palm,
Enter we the army,
  Raise the warrior-psalm;
But for Love that claimeth
  Lives for whom He died:
He whom Jesus nameth
  Must be on His side.
Response. By Thy love constraining,
        By Thy grace divine,
      We are on the Lord's side;
        Saviour, we are Thine.

Jesus, Thou hast bought us,
  Not with gold or gem,
But with Thine own life-blood,

For Thy diadem.
With Thy blessing filling
    Each who comes to Thee,
Thou hast made us willing,
    Thou hast made us free.
Response. By Thy grand redemption,
        By Thy grace divine,
      We are on the Lord's side;
        Saviour, we are Thine.

Fierce may be the conflict,
    Strong may be the foe,
But the King's own army
    None can overthrow.
Round His standard ranging,
    Victory is secure,
For His truth unchanging
    Makes the triumph sure.
Response. Joyfully enlisting
        By Thy grace divine,
      We are on the Lord's side;
        Saviour, we are Thine.

Chosen to be soldiers
    In an alien land;
"Chosen, called, and faithful,"
    For our Captain's band;
In the service royal
    Let us not grow cold;
Let us be right loyal,
    Noble, true, and bold.
Response. Master, Thou wilt keep us,
        By Thy grace divine,
      Always on the Lord's side,
        Saviour, always Thine!

LOYAL RESPONSES

PRAISE
AND
THANKSGIVING

For great is the Lord, and

greatly to be praised . . .

I CHRONICLES 16:25

ADORATION

O Master, at Thy feet
I bow in rapture sweet!
Before me, as in darkening glass,
Some glorious outlines pass
Of love, and truth, and holiness and power;
I own them Thine, O Christ, and bless Thee for this hour.

O full of truth and grace
Smile of Jehovah's face!
O tenderest heart of love untold!
Who may Thy praise unfold?
Thee, Saviour, Lord of lords and King of kings,
Well may adoring seraphs hymn with veiling wings.

I have no words to bring
Worthy of Thee, my King,
And yet one anthem in Thy praise
I long, I long to raise;
The heart is full, the eye entranced above,
But words all melt away in silent awe and love.

How can the lip be dumb,
The hand all still and numb,
When Thee the heart doth see and own
Her Lord and God alone?
Tune for Thyself the music of my days,
And open Thou my lips that I may show Thy praise.

Yea, let my whole life be
One anthem unto Thee,
And let the praise of lip and life
Outring all sin and strife.
O Jesus, Master! be Thy name supreme
For heaven and earth the one, the grand, the eternal theme!

THE MINISTRY OF SONG

THANKSGIVING

THANKS be to God! to whom earth owes
    Sunshine and breeze,
The heath-clad hill, the vale's repose,
    Streamlet and seas,
The snowdrop and the summer rose,
    The many-voiced trees.

Thanks for the darkness that reveals
    Night's starry dower;
And for the sable cloud that heals
    Each fevered flower;
And for the rushing storm that peals
    Our weakness and Thy power.

Thanks for the sweetly-lingering might
    In music's tone;
For paths of knowledge, whose calm light
    Is all Thine own;
For thoughts that at the Infinite
    Fold their bright wings alone.

Yet thanks that silence oft may flow
    In dewlike store;
Thanks for the mysteries that show
    How small our lore;
Thanks that we here so little know
    And trust Thee more!

Thanks for the gladness that entwines
    Our path below;
Each sunrise that incarnadines
    The cold, still snow;
Thanks for the light of love which shines
    With brightest earthly glow.

Thanks for the sickness and the grief
    Which none may flee;
For loved ones standing now around
    The crystal sea;
And for the weariness of heart
    Which only rests in Thee.

Thanks for Thine own thrice-blessed Word,
    And sabbath rest;
Thanks for the hope of glory stored
    In mansions blest;
Thanks for the Spirit's comfort poured
    Into the trembling breast.

Thanks, more than thanks, to Him ascend,
    Who died to win
Our life, and every trophy rend
    From Death and Sin;
Till, when the thanks of Earth shall end,
    The thanks of Heaven begin.

THE MINISTRY OF SONG

THREEFOLD PRAISE
Haydn — Mendelssohn — Handel
"We bless Thee for our creation, preservation, and all the blessings of this life; but above all, for Thine inestimable love in the redemption of the world by our Lord Jesus Christ." Book of Common Prayer

PART I: HAYDN'S *Creation*

WHAT is the first and simplest praise,
    The universal debt,
Which yet the thoughtless heart of man
    So quickly may forget?
"We bless Thee for creation!"
    So taught the noble band
Who left a sound and holy form,
    For ages yet to stand,
Rich legacy of praise and prayer,
    Laid up through ages past,
Strong witness for the truth of God:
    Oh, may we hold it fast!

"We bless Thee for creation!"
    So we are blithely taught
By Haydn's joyous spirit;
    Such was the praise he brought.
A praise all morning sunshine,
    And sparklets of the spring,
O'er which the long life-shadows
    No chastening softness fling.

A praise of early freshness,
    Of carol and of trill,
Re-echoing all the music
    Of valley and of rill.

A praise that we are sharing
    With every singing breeze,
With nightingales and linnets,
    With waterfalls and trees;
With anthems of the flowers,
    Too delicate and sweet
For all their fairy minstrelsy
    Our mortal ears to greet.

A mighty song of blessing
    Archangels too uplift,
For their own bright existence,
    A grand and glorious gift.
But such their full life-chalice,
    So sparkling and so pure,
And such their vivid sense of joy,
    Sweet, solid, and secure,
We cannot write the harmonies
    To such a song of bliss,
We only catch the melody,
    And sing, content with this.

We are but little children,
    And earth a broken toy:
We do not know the treasures
    In our Father's house of joy.
Thanksgivings for creation
    We ignorantly raise;
We know not yet the thousandth part
    Of that for which we praise.

Yet, praise Him for creation!
    Nor cease the happy song,
But this our Hallelujah
    Through all our life prolong;
'Twill mingle with the chorus
    Before the heavenly throne,
Where what it truly is TO BE
    Shall first be fully known.

PART II: MENDELSSOHN'S *Elijah*

O Felix! happy in thy varied store
Of harmonies undreamt before,
How different was the gift
Of praise 'twas thine to pour,
Whether in stately calm, or tempest strong and swift!

Mark the day,
In mourning robe of grey,
Of shrouded mountain and of storm-swept vale,
And purple pall spread o'er the distance pale,
While thunderous masses wildly drift
In lurid gloom and grandeur: then a swift
And dazzling ray bursts through a sudden rift;
The dark waves glitter as the storms subside,
And all is light and glory at the eventide.

O sunlight of thanksgiving! Who that knows
Its bright forth-breaking after dreariest days,
Would change the after-thought of woes
For memory's loveliest light that glows,
If so he must forego one note of the sweet praise?

For not the song
Which knows no minor cadence, sad and long;
And not the tide
Whose emerald and silver pride
Was never dashed in wild and writhing fray,
Where grim and giant rocks hurl back the spray;
And not the crystal atmosphere,
That carves each outline sharp and clear
Upon a sapphire sky: not these, not these,
Nor aught existing but to charm and please,
Without acknowledging life's mystery,
And all the mighty reign
Of yearning and of pain
That fills its half-read history,

Fit music can supply
To lift the wandering heart on high
To that Preserving Love, which rules all change,
And gives "all blessings of this life," so dream-like and so strange.
And his was praise
Deeper and truer, such as those may raise
Who know both shade and sunlight, and whose life
Hath learnt victorious strife
Of courage and of trust and hope still dear,
With passion and with grief, with danger and with fear.

Upriseth now a cry,
Plaintive and piercing, to the brazen sky:
Help, Lord! the harvest days are gone;
Help, Lord! for other help is none;
The infant children cry for bread,
And no man breaketh it. The suckling's tongue for thirst
Now cleaveth to his mouth. Our land is cursed;
Our wasted Zion mourns, in vain her hands are spread.

A mother's tale of grief,
Of sudden blight upon the chief,
The *only* flower of love that cheered her widowed need:
O loneliest! O desolate indeed!
Were it not mockery to whisper here
A word of hope and cheer?

A mountain brow, an awe-struck crowd,
The prayer-sent flame, the prayer-sent cloud,
A mighty faith, a more than kingly power,
Changed for depression's darkest hour;
For one lone shadow in the desert sought
A fainting frame, a spirit overwrought,
A sense of labour vain, and strength all spent for nought.

Death hovering near,
With visible terror-spear
Of famine, or a murder-stained sword,
A stricken land forsaken of her Lord;
While, bowed with doubled fear,

The faithful few appear;
O sorrows manifold outpoured!
Is blessing built upon such dark foundation?
And can a temple rising from such woe,
Rising upon such mournful crypts below,
Be filled with light and joy and sounding adoration?
O strange mosaic! wondrously inlaid
Are all its depths of shade,
With beauteous stones of promise, marbles fair
Of trust and calm, and flashing brightly, there
The precious gems of praise are set, and shine
Resplendent with a light that almost seems Divine.

Thanks be to God!
The thirsty land he laveth,
The perishing He saveth;
The floods lift up their voices,
The answering earth rejoices.
Thanks be to Him, and never-ending laud,
For this new token of His bounteous love,
Who reigns in might the waterfloods above:
The gathering waters rush along;
And leaps the exultant shout, one cataract of song,
Thanks be to God!

Thus joyously we sing;
Nor is this all the praise we bring.
We need not wait for earthquake, storm, and fire
To lift our praises higher;
Nor wait for heaven-dawn ere we join the hymn
Of throne-surrounding cherubim;
For even on earth their anthem hath begun,
To Him, the Mighty and the Holy One.
We know the still small Voice in many a word
Of guidance, and command, and promise heard;
And, knowing it, we bow before His feet,
With love and awe the seraph-strain repeat,
Holy, Holy, Holy! God the Lord!
His glory fills the earth, His name be all-adored.

O Lord, our Lord! how excellent Thy name
Throughout this universal frame;
Therefore Thy children rest
Beneath the shadow of Thy wings,
A shelter safe and blest;
And tune their often tremulous strings
Thy love to praise, Thy glory to proclaim,
The Merciful, the Gracious One, eternally the Same.

PART III: HANDEL'S *Messiah*

HUSH! for a master harp is tuned again,
In truest unison with choirs above,
For prelude to a loftier, sweeter strain,
The praise of God's inestimable love;
Who sent redemption to a world of woe,
That all a Father's heart His banished ones might know.

Hush! while on silvery wing of holiest song
Floats forth the old, dear story of our peace, —
His coming, the Desire of Ages long,
To wear our chains, and win our glad release,
Our wandering joy, to hear such tidings blest,
Is crowned with "Come to Him, and He will give you rest."
Rest, by His sorrow! Bruised for our sin,
Behold the Lamb of God! His death our life.
Now lift your heads, ye gates! He entereth in,
Christ risen indeed, and Conqueror in the strife.
Thanks, thanks to Him who won, and Him who gave
Such victory of love, such triumph o'er the grave.

Hark! "Hallelujah!" O sublimest strain!
Is it prophetic echo of the day
When He, our Saviour and our King, shall reign,
And all the earth shall own His Righteous sway?
Lift heart and voice, and swell the mighty chords,
While hallelujahs peal to Him, the Lord of lords!

"Worthy of all adoration
    Is the Lamb that once was slain,"
Cry, in raptured exultation,
His redeemed from every nation;
    Angel myriads join the strain,
Sounding from their sinless strings
Glory to the King of kings;
Harping, with their harps of gold,
Praise which never can be told.

Hallelujahs full and swelling
    Rise around His throne of might,
All our highest laud excelling;
Holy and Immortal, dwelling
    In the unapproached light,
He is worthy to receive
All that heaven and earth can give;
Blessing, honour, glory, might,
All are His by glorious right.

As the sound of many waters
    Let the full Amen arise!
HALLELUJAH! Ceasing never,
Sounding through the great FOR EVER,
    Linking all its harmonies;
Through eternities of bliss,
Lord, our rapture shall be this,
And our endless life shall be
One AMEN of praise to Thee.

THE MINISTRY OF SONG

[59]

HITHERTO AND HENCEFORTH

Hitherto the Lord hath helped us,
    Guiding all the way;
Henceforth let us trust him fully,
    Trust Him all the day.

Hitherto the Lord hath loved us,
    Caring for His own;
Henceforth let us love Him better,
    Live for Him alone.

Hitherto the Lord hath blessed us,
    Crowning all our days;
Henceforth let us live to bless Him,
    Live to show His praise.

THREEFOLD PRAISE

PRECIOUS THINGS

O what shining revelation of His treasures God hath given!
Precious things of grace and glory, precious things of earth and
      heaven.
Holy Spirit, now unlock them with Thy mighty golden key,
Royal jewels of the kingdom let us now adoring see!

Christ is precious, O most precious, gift of God the Father sealed;
Pearl of greatest price and treasure, hidden, yet to us revealed;
His own people's crown of glory, and resplendent diadem;
More than thousand worlds, and dearer than all life and love to
      them.   *I Peter 2:7*

Marvellous and very precious is the Corner Stone Elect;
Though rejected by the builders, chosen by the Architect;
All-supporting, all-uniting, and all-crowning, tried and sure;
True Foundation, yet true Headstone of His temple bright and
      pure.   *I Peter 2:6*

Now, in reverent love and wonder, touch the theme of deepest laud,
Precious blood of Christ that bought us and hath made us nigh to
      God!
His own blood, O love unfathomed! shed for those who loved Him
      not;
Mighty fountain always open, cleansing us from every spot.
      I Peter 1:18, 19

O how wonderful and precious are Thy thoughts to us, O God!
Outlined in Creation, blazoned on Redemption's banner broad;
Infinite and deep and dazzling as the noontide heavens above;
Yet more wonderful to usward are Thy thoughts of peace and
      love.   *Psalm 139:17*

Then, exceeding great and precious are Thy promises Divine;
Given by Christ, and by the Spirit sealed with sweetest "All are
thine!"
Precious in their peace and power, in their sure and changeless
might,
Strengthening, comforting, transforming; suns by day and stars by
night.   *II Peter 1:4*

Precious faith our God hath given; rich in faith is rich indeed!
Fire-tried gold from His own treasury, fully meeting every need:
Channel of His grace abounding; bringing peace and joy and light;
Purifying, overcoming, linking weakness with His might.
    II Peter 1:1

Precious ointment, very costly, of chief odours pure and sweet,
Holy gift for royal priesthood, thus for temple-service meet;
Such the Spirit's precious unction, oil of gladness freely shed,
Sanctifying and abiding on the consecrated head.   *Psalm 133:2*

Who shall paint the flash of splendour from the opened casket
bright,
When His precious lovingkindness beams upon the quickened
sight!
Priceless jewel ever gleaming with imperishable ray,
God will never take it from us, though the mountains pass
away.   *Psalm 36:7; Isaiah 54:8, 10*

Far more precious than the ruby, or the crystal's rainbow light,
Valued not with precious onyx or with pearl and sapphire bright,
Freely given to all who ask it, is the wisdom from above,
Pure and peaceable and gentle, full of fruits of life and love.
    Job 28:16, 18

Nor withhold we glad thanksgiving for His mercies ever new,
Precious things of earth and heaven, sun and rain and quickening
dew;
Precious fruits and varied crowning of the year His goodness fills,
Chief things of the ancient mountains, precious things of lasting
hills.   *Deuteronomy 33:13-16*

Such His gifts! but mark we duly our responsibility
Unto Him whose name is Holy, infinite in purity;
Sin and self no longer serving, take the precious from the vile,
So His power shall rest upon thee, thou shalt dwell beneath His
      smile.   *Jeremiah 15:19*

Sons of Zion, ye are precious in your heavenly Father's sight,
Ye are His peculiar treasure, ye are His jewels of delight;
Sought and chosen, cleansed and polished, purchased with
      transcendent cost,
Kept in His own royal casket, never, never to be lost.
    Lamentations 4:2

Precious, more than gold that wasteth, is the trial of your faith,
Fires of anguish or temptation cannot dim it, cannot scathe!
Your Refiner sitteth watching till His image shineth clear,
For His glory, praise, and honour, when the Saviour shall appear.
    I Peter 1:7

Precious, precious to Jehovah is His children's holy sleep;
He is with them in the passing through the waters cold and deep;
Everlasting love enfolds them softly, safely to His breast,
Everlasting love receives them to His glory and His rest.
    Psalm 116:15

Pause not here, — the Holy City, glorious in God's light, behold!
Like unto a stone most precious, clear as crystal, pure as gold;
Strong foundations, fair with sapphires, sardius and chrysolite,
Blent with amethyst and jacinth, emerald and topaz bright.
    Revelations 21:10, 11

Glorious dwelling of the holy, where no grief or gloom of sin
Through the pure and pearly portals evermore shall enter in:
Christ its Light and God its Temple, Christ its song of endless laud!
O what precious consummation of the precious things of
      God.   *Hebrews 11:10*

UNDER HIS SHADOW

THE INFINITY OF GOD

Too wonderful for me.
Psalm 139:6

HOLY and Infinite! Viewless, Eternal!
    Veiled in the glory that none can sustain,
None comprehendeth Thy being supernal,
    Nor can the heaven of heavens contain.

Holy and Infinite! limitless, boundless,
    All Thy perfections, and power, and praise!
Oceans of mystery! awful and soundless
    All Thine unsearchable judgment and ways!

King of Eternity! what revelation
    Could the created and finite sustain,
But for Thy marvellous manifestation,
    Godhead incarnate in weakness and pain!

Therefore archangels and angels adore Thee,
    Seraphim, cherubim love and admire;
Therefore we praise Thee, rejoicing before Thee,
    Joining in rapture the heavenly choir.

Glorious in holiness, fearful in praises,
    Who shall not fear Thee, and who shall not laud?
Anthems of glory Thy universe raises,
    Holy and Infinite! Father and God!

UNDER THE SURFACE

THE SPIRITUALITY OF GOD

God is a spirit.
John 4:24

WHAT know we, Holy God, of Thee,
    Thy being and Thine essence pure?
Too bright the very mystery
    For mortal vision to endure.

We only know Thy word sublime,
    Thou art a Spirit! Perfect! One!
Unlimited by space or time,
    Unknown but through the eternal Son.

By change untouched, by thought untraced,
    And by created eye unseen,
In Thy great Present is embraced
    All that shall be, all that hath been.

O Father of our spirits, now
    We seek Thee in our Saviour's face;
In truth and spirit we would bow,
    And worship where we cannot trace.

UNDER THE SURFACE

THE ETERNITY OF GOD

*The King eternal, immortal,
invisible.* I Timothy 1:17

KING Eternal and Immortal!
  We, the children of an hour,
Bend in lowly adoration,
Rise in raptured admiration,
   At the whisper of Thy power.
    Myriad ages in Thy sight
     Are but as the fleeting day;
    Like a vision of the night,
     Worlds may rise and pass away.

All Thy glories are eternal,
  None shall ever pass away;
Truth and mercy all victorious,
Righteousness and love all glorious,
   Shine with everlasting ray:
    All resplendent, ere the light
     Bade primeval darkness flee;
    All transcendent, through the flight
     Of eternities to be.

Thou art God from everlasting,
  And to everlasting art!
Ere the dawn of shadowy ages,
Dimly guessed by angel sages,
   Ere the beat of seraph-heart,
    Thou Jehovah, art the same,
     And Thy years shall have no end;
    Changeless nature, changeless name,
     Ever Father, God, and Friend!

UNDER THE SURFACE

THE SOVEREIGNTY OF GOD

Be still and know that I am God.
Psalm 46:10

GOD Almighty! King of nations! earth Thy footstool, heaven
    Thy throne!
Thine the greatness, power, and glory; Thine the kingdom,
    Lord, alone!
Life and death are in Thy keeping, and Thy will ordaineth all,
From the armies of Thy heavens to an unseen insect's fall.

Reigning, guiding, all-commanding, ruling myriad worlds of light;
Now exalting, now abasing, none can stay Thy hand of might!
Working all things by Thy power, by the counsel of Thy will,
Thou art God! enough to know it, and to hear Thy word: "Be still!"

In Thy sovereignty rejoicing, we Thy children bow and praise,
For we know that kind and loving, just and true, are all Thy ways.
While Thy heart of sovereign mercy and Thine arm of sovereign
        might,
For our great and strong salvation, in Thy sovereign grace unite.

UNDER THE SURFACE

OUR KING

Worship thou Him.
Psalm 45:11

O Saviour, precious Saviour,
  Whom yet unseen we love!
O Name of might and favour,
  All other names above!
    We worship Thee, we bless Thee,
      To Thee alone we sing;
    We praise Thee, and confess Thee
      Our holy Lord and King!

O Bringer of salvation,
  Who wondrously hast wrought,
Thyself the revelation
  Of love beyond our thought:
    We worship Thee, we bless Thee,
      To Thee alone we sing;
    We praise Thee, and confess Thee
      Our gracious Lord and King!

In Thee all fulness dwelleth,
  All grace and power divine;
The glory that excelleth,
  O son of God, is Thine:
    We worship Thee, we bless Thee,
      To Thee alone we sing;
    We praise Thee, and confess Thee
      Our glorious Lord and King!

Oh, grant the consummation
  Of this our song above,

In endless adoration,
    And everlasting love:
        Then shall we praise and bless Thee,
            Where perfect praises ring,
        And evermore confess Thee
            Our Saviour and our King!

UNDER THE SURFACE

CHOSEN IN CHRIST

He hath chosen us in Him
before the foundation of
the world. Ephesians 1:4

O Thou chosen Church of Jesus, glorious, blessed, and secure,
Founded on the One Foundation, which for ever shall endure;
Not thy holiness or beauty can thy strength and safety be,
But the everlasting love wherewith Jehovah loved thee.

Chosen — by His own good pleasure, by the counsel of His will,
Mystery of power and wisdom working for His people still;
Chosen — in thy mighty Saviour, ere one ray of quickening light
Beamed upon the chaos, waiting for the Word of sovereign might.

Chosen — through the Holy Spirit, through the sanctifying grace
Poured upon His precious vessels, meetened for the heavenly place;
Chosen — to show forth His praises, to be holy in His sight;
Chosen — unto grace and glory, chosen unto life and light.

Blessed be the God and Father of our Saviour Jesus Christ,
Who hath blessed us with such blessings, all uncounted and
          unpriced!
Let our high and holy calling, and our strong salvation, be
Theme of never-ending praises, God of sovereign grace, to Thee!

UNDER THE SURFACE

SINGING FOR JESUS

With my song will I praise Him.
Psalm 28:7

SINGING for Jesus, our Saviour and King,
    Singing for Jesus, the Lord whom we love;
All adoration we joyously bring,
    Longing to praise as we praise Him above.

Singing for Jesus, our Master and Friend,
    Telling His love and His marvellous grace;
Love from eternity, love without end,
    Love for the loveless, the sinful and base.

Singing for Jesus, and trying to win
    Many to love Him, and join in the song;
Calling the weary and wandering in,
    Rolling the chorus of gladness along.

Singing for Jesus, our Life and our Light,
    Singing for Him as we press to the mark;
Singing for Him when the morning is bright,
    Singing, still singing, for Him in the dark.

Singing for Jesus, our Shepherd and Guide,
    Singing for gladness of heart that He gives;
Singing for wonder and praise that He died,
    Singing for blessing and joy that He lives.

Singing for Jesus, oh, singing with joy!
    Thus will we praise Him and tell out His love,
Till He shall call us to brighter employ,
    Singing for Jesus for ever above.

UNDER THE SURFACE

TRUSTING
GOD

*O taste and see that the Lord
is good; blessed is the man
that trusteth in him.* PSALM 34:8

WHAT WILL YOU DO WITHOUT HIM?

I could not do without Him!
　　Jesus is more to me
Than all the richest, fairest gifts
　　Of earth could ever be.
But the more I find Him precious —
　　And the more I find Him true —
The more I long for you to find
　　What He can be to you.

You need not do without Him,
　　For He is passing by,
He is waiting to be gracious,
　　Only waiting for your cry;
He is waiting to receive you —
　　To make you all His own!
Why will you do without Him,
　　And wander on alone?

Why will you do without Him?
　　Is He not kind indeed?
Did He not die to save you?
　　Is He not all you need?
Do you not want a Saviour?
　　Do you not want a Friend?
One who will love you faithfully,
　　And love you to the end?

Why will you do without Him?
　　The Word of God is true,

The world is passing to its doom —
    And you are passing too.
It may be no tomorrow
    Shall dawn on you or me;
Why will you run the awful risk
    Of all eternity?

What will you do without Him,
    In the long and dreary day
Of trouble and perplexity,
    When you do not know the way,
And no one else can help you,
    And no one guides you right,
And hope comes not with morning,
    And rest comes not with night?

You could not do without Him,
    If once He made you see
The fetters that enchain you,
    Till He hath set you free.
If once you saw the fearful load
    Of sin upon your soul —
The hidden plague that ends in death,
    Unless He makes you whole.

What will you do without Him
    When death is drawing near?
Without His love — the only love
    That casts out every fear;
When the shadow-valley opens,
    Unlighted and unknown,
And the terrors of its darkness
    Must all be passed alone!

What will you do without Him,
    When the great white throne is set,
And the Judge who never can mistake,
    And never can forget, —
The Judge whom you have never here

As Friend and Saviour sought,
        Shall summon you to give account
        Of deed and word and thought?

What will you do without Him,
        When He hath shut the door,
And you are left outside, because
        You would not come before?
When it is no use knocking,
        No use to stand and wait,
For the word of doom tolls through your heart,
        That terrible "Too late!"

You *cannot* do without Him!
        There is no other Name
By which you ever *can* be saved,
        No way, no hope, no claim!
Without Him — everlasting loss
        Of love, and life, and light!
Without Him — everlasting woe,
        And everlasting night.

But with Him — oh! *with Jesus!*
        Are any words so blest?
With Jesus, everlasting joy
        And everlasting rest!
With Jesus, — all the empty heart
        Filled with His perfect love;
With Jesus, — perfect peace below,
        And perfect bliss above.

Why should you do without Him?
        It is not yet too late;
He has not closed the day of grace,
        He has not shut the gate.
He calls you! — hush! He calls you!
        He would not have you go
Another step without Him,
        Because He loves you so.

He would not do without you!
He calls and calls again —
"Come unto Me! Come unto Me!"
Oh, shall He call in vain?
He wants to have you with Him;
Do you not want Him too?
You cannot do without Him,
And He wants — even you.

UNDER HIS SHADOW

THE SECRET OF A HAPPY DAY

*The secret of the Lord
is with them that fear
Him.* Psalm 25:14

JUST to let thy Father do
  What He will;
Just to know that He is true,
  And be still.
Just to follow hour by hour
  As He leadeth;
Just to draw the moment's power
  As it needeth.
Just to trust Him, this is all!
  Then the day will surely be
Peaceful, whatsoe'er befall,
  Bright and blessed, calm and free.

Just to let Him speak to thee
  Through His word,
Watching, that His voice may be
  Clearly heard.
Just to tell Him everything
  As it rises,
And at once to Him to bring
  All surprises.
Just to listen, and to stay
  Where you cannot miss His voice.
This is all! and thus today,
  Communing, you shall rejoice.

Just to ask Him what to do
  All the day,

And to make you quick and true
  To obey.
Just to know the needed grace
  He bestoweth,
Every bar of time and place
  Overfloweth.
Just to take thy order straight
  From the Master's own command!
Blessed day! when thus we wait
  Always at our Sovereign's hand.

Just to recollect His love
  Always true;
Always shining from above,
  Always new.
Just to recognise its light
  All-enfolding;
Just to claim its present might,
  All-upholding.
Just to know it as thine own,
  That no power can take away.
Is not this enough alone
  For the gladness of the day?

Just to trust, and yet to ask
  Guidance still;
Take the training, or the task,
  As He will.
Just to take the loss or gain,
  As He sends it.
He who formed thee for His praise
  Will not miss the gracious aim;
So today and all thy days
  Shall be moulded for the same.

Just to leave in His dear hand
  Little things,
All we cannot understand,
  All that stings!
Just to let Him take the care

Sorely pressing,
Finding all we let Him bear
Changed to blessing.
This is all! and yet the way
Marked by Him who loves thee best!
Secret of a happy day,
Secret of His promised rest.

LOYAL RESPONSES

TRUSTING JESUS

I am trusting Thee, Lord Jesus,
　　Trusting only Thee;
Trusting Thee for full salvation,
　　Great and free.

I am trusting Thee for pardon;
　　At Thy feet I bow,
For Thy grace and tender mercy,
　　Trusting now.

I am trusting Thee for cleansing
　　In the crimson flood;
Trusting Thee to make me holy
　　By Thy blood.

I am trusting Thee to guide me;
　　Thou alone shalt lead!
Every day and hour supplying
　　All my need.

I am trusting Thee for power;
　　Thine can never fail!
Words which Thou Thyself shalt give me,
　　Must prevail.

I am trusting Thee, Lord Jesus:
　　Never let me fall!
I am trusting Thee for ever,
　　And for all.

LOYAL RESPONSES

BE NOT WEARY

YES! He knows the way is dreary,
    Knows the weakness of our frame,
Knows that hand and heart are weary;
    He, "in all points," felt the same.
He is near to help and bless;
Be not weary, onward press.

Look to Him who once was willing
    All His glory to resign,
That, for thee the law fulfilling,
    All His merit might be thine.
Strive to follow day by day
Where His footsteps mark the way.

Look to Him, the Lord of glory,
    Tasting death to win thy life;
Gazing on that "wondrous story,"
    Canst thou falter in the strife?
Is it not new life to know
That the Lord hath loved thee so?

Look to Him who ever liveth,
    Interceding for His own;
Seek yea, claim the grace He giveth
    Freely from His priestly throne.
Will He not thy strength renew
With His Spirit's quickening dew?

Look to Him, and faith shall brighten,
    Hope shall soar, and love shall burn;
Peace once more thy heart shall lighten;

Rise! He calleth thee! return!
Be not weary on thy way,
Jesus is thy strength and stay.

THE MINISTRY OF SONG

WITHOUT CAREFULNESS

I would have you
without carefulness.
I Corinthians 7:32

MASTER! how shall I bless Thy name
    For Thy tender love to me.
For the sweet enablings of Thy grace,
    So sovereign, yet so free,
That have taught me to obey Thy word
    And cast my care on Thee!

They tell of weary burdens borne
    For discipline of life,
Of long anxieties and doubts,
    Of struggle and of strife,
Of a path of dim perplexities
    With fears and shadows rife.

Oh, I have trod that weary path,
    With burdens not a few,
With shadowy faith that Thou wouldst lead
    And help me safely through,
Trying to follow and obey,
    And bear my burdens too.

Master! dear Master, Thou didst speak,
    And yet I did not hear,
Or long ago I might have ceased
    From every care and fear,
And gone rejoicing on my way
    From brightening year to year.

Just now and then some steeper slope
    Would seem so hard to climb,
That I *must* cast my load on Thee;
    And I left it for a time,
And wondered at the joy at heart,
    Like sweetest Christmas chime.

A step or two on winged feet,
    And then I turned to share
The burden Thou hadst taken up
    Of ever-pressing care;
So what I would not leave with Thee
    Of course I had to bear.

At last Thy precious precepts fell
    On opened heart and ear,
A varied and repeated strain
    I could not choose but hear,
Enlinking promise and command,
    Like harp and clarion clear:

"No anxious thought upon thy brow
    The watching world should see;
No carefulness! O child of God,
    For *nothing* careful be!
But cast thou *all* thy care on Him
    Who always cares for thee."

Did not Thy loving Spirit come
    In gentle, precious shower,
To work Thy pleasure in my soul
    In that bright, blessed hour,
And to the word of strong command
    Add faith and will and power?

It was Thy word, it was Thy will —
    That was enough for me!

Henceforth no care shall dim my trust,
　　For all is cast on Thee;
Henceforth my inmost heart shall praise
　　The grace that set me free.

And now I find Thy promise true,
　　Of perfect peace and rest;
I cannot sigh — I can but sing
　　While leaning on thy breast,
And leaving everything to Thee,
　　Whose ways are always best.

I never thought it could be thus, —
　　Month after month to know
The river of Thy peace without
　　One ripple in its flow;
Without one quiver in the trust,
　　One flicker in its glow.

Oh, Thou hast done far more for me
　　Than I had asked or thought!
I stand and marvel to behold
　　What Thou, my Lord, hast wrought,
And wonder what glad lessons yet
　　I shall be daily taught.

How shall I praise Thee, Saviour dear,
　　For this new life so sweet,
For taking all the care I laid
　　At Thy beloved feet,
Keeping Thy hand upon my heart
　　To still each anxious beat!

I want to praise, with life renewed,
　　As I never praised before;
With voice and pen, with song and speech,
　　To praise Thee more and more,

And the gladness and the gratitude
    Rejoicingly outpour.

I long to praise Thee more, and yet
    This is no care to me:
If Thou shalt fill my mouth with songs,
    Then I will sing to Thee;
And if my silence praise Thee best,
    Then silent I will be.

Yet if it be Thy will, dear Lord,
    Oh, send me forth, to be
Thy messenger to careful hearts,
    To bid them taste and see
How good Thou art to those who cast
    All, all their care on Thee!

LOYAL RESPONSES

NOT YET

John 13:7

NOT yet thou knowest what I do,
    O feeble child of earth,
Whose life is but to angel view
    The morning of thy birth!
The smallest leaf, the simplest flower,
    The wild bee's honey-cell,
Have lessons of My love and power
    Too hard for thee to spell.

Thou knowest not how I uphold
    The little thou dost scan;
And how much less canst thou unfold
    My universal plan,
Where all thy mind can grasp of space
    Is but a grain of sand; —
The time thy boldest thought can trace,
    One ripple on the strand!

Not yet thou knowest what I do
    In this wild, warring world,
Whose prince doth still triumphant view
    Confusion's flag unfurled;
Nor how each proud and daring thought
    Is subject to my will,
Each strong and secret purpose brought
    My counsel to fulfil.

Not yet thou knowest how I bid
    Each passing hour entwine
Its grief or joy, its hope or fear,
    In one great love-design;
Nor how I lead thee through the night,
    By many a various way,
Still upward to unclouded light,
    And onward to the day.

Not yet thou knowest what I do
    Within thine own weak breast,
To mould thee to My image true,
    And fit thee for My rest.
But yield thee to My loving skill;
    The veiled work of grace,
From day to day progressing still,
    It is not thine to trace.

Yes, walk by faith and not by sight,
    Fast clinging to My hand;
Content to feel My love and might,
    Not yet to understand.
A little while thy course pursue,
    Till grace to glory grow;
Then what I am, and what I do,
    Hereafter thou shalt know.

THE MINISTRY OF SONG

A GREAT MYSTERY

THERE is a hush in earth and sky,
    The ear is free to list aright
In darkness, veiling from the eye
    The many-coloured spells of light.

Not heralded by fire and storm,
    In shadowy outline dimly seen,
Comes through the gloom a glorious Form,
    The once despised Nazarene.

Through waiting silence, voiceless shade,
    A still, small Voice so clearly floats,
A listening lifetime were o'erpaid
    By one sweet echo of such notes.

"Fear not, beloved! thou art Mine,
    For I have given My life for thee;
By name I call thee, rise and shine,
    Be praise and glory unto Me.

"In Me all spotless and complete,
    And in My comeliness most fair
Art thou; to Me thy voice is sweet,
    Prevailing in thy feeblest prayer.

"Thy life is hid in God with Me,
    I stoop to dwell within thy breast;

DISAPPOINTMENT

Our yet unfinished story
   Is tending all to this:
To God the greatest glory,
   To us the greatest bliss.

If all things work together
   For ends so grand and blest,
What need to wonder whether
   Each in itself is best?

If some things were omitted
   Or altered as we would,
The whole might be unfitted
   To work for perfect good.

We cannot see before us,
   But our all-seeing Friend
Is always watching o'er us,
   And knows the very end.

What though we seem to stumble?
   He will not let us fall;
And learning to be humble
   Is not lost time at all.

And when amid our blindness
   His disappointments fall,

We trust His lovingkindness
     Whose wisdom sends them all.

They are the purple fringes
     That hide His glorious feet;
They are the fire-wrought hinges
     Where truth and mercy meet:

By them the golden portal
     Of Providence shall ope,
And lift to praise immortal
     The songs of faith and hope.

From broken alabaster
     Was deathless fragrance shed,
The spikenard flowed the faster
     Upon the Saviour's head.

No shattered box of ointment
     We ever need regret,
For out of disappointment
     Flow sweetest odours yet.

The discord that involveth
     Some startling change of key,
The Master's hand resolveth
     In richest harmony.

We hush our children's laughter
     When sunset hues grow pale;
Then, in the silence after,
     They hear the nightingale.

We mourned the lamp declining,
     That glimmered at our side; —
The glorious starlight shining
     Has proved a surer guide.

My joy for ever thou shalt be,
　　And in My love for thee I rest.

"O Prince's daughter, whom I see
　　In bridal garments, pure as light,
Betrothed for ever unto Me,
　　On thee My own new name I write."

Lo! "neath the stars" uncertain ray
　　In flowing mantle glistening fair,
One, lowly bending, turns away
　　From that sweet voice in cold despair.

Is it Humility, who sees
　　Herself unworthy of such grace,
Who dares not hope her Lord to please,
　　Who dares not look upon His face?

Nay, where that mantle fleeting gleams,
　　'Tis Unbelief who turns aside,
Who rather rests in self-spun dreams,
　　Than trust the love of Him who died.

Faith casts away the fair disguise,
　　She will not doubt her Master's voice,
And droop when He hath bid her rise,
　　Or mourn when He hath said, "Rejoice!"

Her stained and soiled robes she leaves,
　　And Christ's own shining raiment takes;
What His love gives, her love receives,
　　And meek and trustful answer makes:

"Behold the handmaid of the Lord!
　　Thou callest, and I come to Thee
According to Thy faithful word,
　　O Master, be it unto me!

"Thy love I cannot comprehend,
    I only know Thy word is true,
And that Thou lovest to the end
    Each whom to Thee the Father drew.

"Oh! take the heart I could not give
    Without Thy strength-bestowing call;
In Thee, and for Thee, let me live.
    For I am nothing, Thou art all."

THE MINISTRY OF SONG

Then tremble not and shrink not
    When Disappointment nears;
Be trustful still, and think not
    To realize all fears.

While we are meekly kneeling,
    We shall behold her rise,
Our Father's love revealing,
    An angel in disguise.

THE MINISTRY OF SONG

FAITH AND REASON

REASON unstrings the harp, to see
    Wherein the music dwells;
Faith pours a Hallelujah song,
    And heavenly rapture swells.
While Reason strives to count the drops
    That lave our narrow strand,
Faith launches o'er the mighty deep,
    To seek a better land.

One is the foot that slowly treads
    Where darkling mists enshroud;
The other is the wing that cleaves
    Each heaven-obscuring cloud.
Reason, the eye which sees but that
    On which its glance is cast;
Faith is the thought that blends in one
    The Future and the Past.

In hours of darkness, Reason waits,
    Like those in days of yore,
Who rose not from their night-bound place
    On dark Egyptian shore.
But Faith more firmly clasps the hand
    Which led her all the day,
And when the wished-for morning dawns,
    Is farther on her way.

By Reason's alchymy [*sic*] in vain
    Is golden treasure planned;
Faith meekly takes a priceless crown,
    Won by no mortal hand.
While Reason is the labouring oar
    That smites the wrathful seas,
Faith is the snowy sail spread out
    To catch the freshening breeze.

Reason, the telescope that scans
    A universe of light;
But Faith, the angel who may dwell
    Among those regions bright.
Reason, a lonely towering elm,
    May fall before the blast;
Faith, like the ivy on the rock,
    Is safe in clinging fast.

While Reason, like a Levite, waits
    Where priest and people meet,
Faith, by a "new and living way,"
    Hath gained the mercy-seat.
While Reason but returns to tell
    That this is not our rest,
Faith, like a weary dove, hath sought
    A gracious Saviour's breast.

Yet both are surely precious gifts
    From Him who leads us home,
Though in the wilds Himself hath trod
    A little while we roam.
And, linked within the soil that knows
    A living, loving Lord,
Faith strikes the key-note, Reason then
    Fills up the full-toned chord.

Faith is the upward-pointing spire
    O'er life's great temple springing,

From which the chimes of love float forth,
 Celestially ringing;
While Reason stands below upon
 The consecrated ground,
And, like a mighty buttress, clasps
 The wide foundation round.

Faith is the bride that stands enrobed
 In white and pure array;
Reason, the handmaid who may share
 The gladness of the day.
Faith leads the way, and Reason learns
 To follow in her train,
Till, step by step, the goal is reached,
 And death is glorious gain.

THE MINISTRY OF SONG

CONFIDENCE

IN Thee I trust, on Thee I rest,
O Saviour dear, Redeemer blest!
No earthly friend, no brother knows
My weariness, my wants, my woes.
    On Thee I call,
    Who knowest all.
O Saviour dear, Redeemer blest,
In Thee I trust, on Thee I rest.

Thy power, Thy love, Thy faithfulness,
With lip and life I long to bless.
Thy faithfulness shall be my tower,
My sun Thy love, my shield Thy power
    In darkest night,
    In fiercest fight.
With lip and life I long to bless
Thy power, Thy love, Thy faithfulness.

THREEFOLD PRAISE

THINE IS THE POWER

OUR Father, our Father, who dwellest in light,
We lean on Thy love, and we rest on Thy might;
In weakness and weariness joy shall abound,
For strength everlasting in Thee shall be found:
Our Refuge, our Helper in conflict and woe,
Our mighty Defender, how blessed to know
    That Thine is the power!

Our Father, Thy promise we earnestly claim,
The sanctified heart that shall hallow Thy Name,
In ourselves, in our dear ones, throughout the wide world,
Be Thy Name as a banner of glory unfurled;
Let it triumph o'er evil and darkness and guilt,
We know Thou canst do it, we know that Thou wilt,
    For Thine is the power!

Our Father, we long for the glorious day
When all shall adore Thee, and all shall obey.
Oh hasten Thy kingdom, oh show forth Thy might,
And wave o'er the nations Thy sceptre of right.
Oh make up Thy jewels, the crown of Thy love,
And reign in our hearts as Thou reignest above.
    For Thine is the power!

Our Father, we pray that Thy will may be done,
For full acquiescence is heaven begun; —
Both in us and by us Thy purpose be wrought,
In word and in action, in spirit and thought;
And Thou canst enable us thus to fulfil,
With holy rejoicing, Thy glorious will,
    For Thine is the power!

Our Father, Thou carest; Thou knowest indeed
Our inmost desires, our manifold need;
The fount of Thy mercies shall never be dry,
For Thy riches in glory shall mete the supply;
Our bread shall be given, our water be sure,
And nothing shall fail, for Thy word shall endure,
    And Thine is the power!

Our Father, forgive us, for we have transgressed,
Have wounded Thy love, and forsaken Thy breast;
In the peace of Thy pardon henceforth let us live,
That through Thy forgiveness we too may forgive;
The Son of Thy love, who hath taught us to pray,
For Thy treasures of mercy hath opened the way,
    And Thine is the power!

Thou knowest our dangers, Thou knowest our frame,
But a tower of strength is Thy glorious name;
Oh, lead us not into temptation, we pray,
But keep us, and let us not stumble or stray;
Thy children shall under Thy shadow abide,
In Thee as our Guide and our Shield we confide,
    For Thine is the power!

Our Father, deliver Thy children from sin,
From evil without and from evil within,
From this world, with its manifold evil and wrong,
From the wiles of the Evil One, subtle and strong;
Till, as Christ overcame, we, too, conquer and sing,
    For Thine is the power!

Our Father, Thy children rejoice in Thy reign,
Rejoice in Thy highness, and praise Thee again!
Yea, Thine is the kingdom and Thine is the might,
And Thine is the glory transcendently bright;
For ever and ever that glory shall shine,
For ever and ever that kingdom be Thine,
    For Thine is the power!

UNDER THE SURFACE

UNDER HIS SHADOW

I sat down under His
shadow with great delight.
Canticles 2:3

SIT down beneath His shadow,
　　And rest with great delight;
The faith that now beholds Him
　　Is pledge of future sight.

Our Master's love remember,
　　Exceeding great and free;
Lift up thy heart in gladness,
　　For He remembers thee.

Bring every weary burden,
　　Thy sin, thy fear, thy grief,
He calls the heavy laden,
　　And gives them kind relief.

His righteousness "all glorious"
　　Thy festal robe shall be;
And love that passeth knowledge,
　　His banner over thee.

A little while though parted,
　　Remember, wait, and love,
Until He comes in glory,
　　Until we meet above;

Till in the Father's kingdom
　　The heavenly feast is spread,
And we behold His beauty,
　　Whose blood for us was shed!

UNDER THE SURFACE

ACKNOWLEDGMENT OF OUR DEBT

Herein is love, not that we loved God, but that he loved us, and sent his Son to be the propitiation for our sins.

I JOHN 4:10

NOTHING TO PAY

NOTHING to pay! Ah, nothing to pay!
Never a word of excuse to say!
Year after year thou hast filled the score,
Owing thy Lord still more and more.
    Hear the voice of Jesus say,
"Verily thou hast nothing to pay!
Ruined, lost are thou, and yet
I forgave thee all that debt."

Nothing to pay! the debt is so great;
What will you do with the awful weight?
How shall the way of escape be made?
Nothing to pay! yet it must be paid!
    Hear the voice of Jesus say,
"Verily thou hast nothing to pay!
All has been put to My account,
I have paid the full amount."

Nothing to pay; yes, nothing to pay!
Jesus has cleared all the debt away;
Blotted it out with His bleeding hand!
Free and forgiven and loved you stand.
    Hear the voice of Jesus say,
"Verily thou hast nothing to pay!
Paid is the debt, and the debtor free!
Now I ask *thee,* lovest thou ME?"

CLOSING CHORDS

BY THY CROSS AND PASSION

He hath given us rest
by His sorrow, and life
by His death. John Bunyan

WHAT hast Thou done for me, O mighty Friend,
  ' Who lovest to the end!
Reveal Thyself, that I may now behold
    Thy love unknown, untold,
Bearing the curse, and made a curse for me,
That blessed and made a blessing I might be.

Oh, Thou wast crowned with thorns, that I might wear
    A crown of glory fair;
"Exceeding sorrowful," that I might be
    Exceeding glad in Thee;
"Rejected and despised," that I might stand
Accepted and complete on Thy right hand.

Wounded for my transgression, stricken sore,
    That I might "sin no more;"
Weak, that I might be always strong in Thee;
    Bound, that I might be free;
Acquaint with grief, that I might only know
Fulness of joy in everlasting flow.

Thine was the chastisement, with no release,
    That mine might be the peace;
The bruising and the cruel stripes were Thine,
    That healing might be mine;
Thine was the sentence and the condemnation,
Mine the acquittal and the full salvation.

For Thee revilings, and a mocking throng,
    For me the angel-song;
For Thee the frown, the hiding of God's face,
    For me His smile of grace;
Sorrows of hell and bitterest death for Thee,
And heaven and everlasting life for me.

Thy cross and passion, and Thy precious death,
    While I have mortal breath,
Shall be my spring of love and work and praise,
    The life of all my days;
Till all this mystery of love supreme
Be solved in glory — glory's endless theme.

LOYAL RESPONSES

THE PRECIOUS BLOOD OF JESUS

PRECIOUS, precious blood of Jesus,
    Shed on Calvary;
Shed for rebels, shed for sinners,
    Shed for me.

Precious blood, that hath redeemed us!
    All the price is paid;
Perfect pardon now is offered,
    Peace is made.

Precious, precious blood of Jesus,
    Let it make thee whole
Let it flow in mighty cleansing
    O'er thy soul.

Though thy sins are red like crimson,
    Deep in scarlet glow,
Jesu's precious blood can make them
    White as snow.

Now the holiest with boldness
    We may enter in,
For the open fountain cleanseth
    From all sin.

Precious blood! by this we conquer
    In the fiercest fight,

Sin and Satan overcoming
    By its might.

Precious, precious blood of Jesus,
    Ever flowing free!
O believe it, O receive it,
    'Tis for thee.

Precious blood, whose full atonement
    Makes us nigh to God!
Precious blood, our song of glory,
    Praise and laud!

LOYAL RESPONSES

PRESENTED FAULTLESS

Behold I and the children
which God hath given Me.
Hebrews 2:13

OUR Saviour and our King,
　　Enthroned and crowned above,
Shall with exceeding gladness bring
　　The children of His love.

All that the Father gave
　　His glory shall behold;
Not one whom Jesus came to save
　　Is missing from His fold.

He shall confess His own,
　　From every clime and coast,
Before His Father's glorious throne,
　　Before the angel host.

"O righteous Father, see,
　　In spotless robes arrayed,
Thy chosen gifts of love to Me,
　　Before the worlds were made.

"As Thou hast loved Me,
　　So hast Thou loved them;
Thy precious jewels they shall be,
　　My glorious diadem!"

UNDER THE SURFACE

HE SUFFERED

"HE suffered!" Was it, Lord, indeed for me,
    The Just One for the unjust, Thou didst bear
    The weight of sorrow that I hardly dare
To look upon, in dark Gethsemane?
"He suffered!" Thou, my near and gracious Friend,
    And yet my Lord, my God! Thou didst not shrink
    For me that full and fearful cup to drink,
Because Thou lovedst even to the end!
"He suffered!" Saviour, was Thy love so vast,
    That mysteries of unknown agony,
    Even unto death, its only gauge could be,
Unmeasured as the fiery depths it passed?
Lord, by the sorrows of Gethsemane,
Seal Thou my quivering love for ever unto Thee!

CLOSING CHORDS

I DID THIS FOR THEE!
WHAT HAST THOU DONE FOR ME?

I gave My life for thee,   *Gal. 2:20*
    My precious blood I shed,   *I Pet. 1:19*
That thou might'st ransomed be,   *Eph. 1:7*
    And quickened from the dead.   *Eph. 2:1*
I gave My life for thee;   *Tit. 2:14*
What hast thou given Me?   *John 21:15-17*

I spent long years for thee   *I Tim. 1:15*
    In weariness and woe,   *Isa. 53:3*
That an eternity   *John 17:24*
    Of joy thou mightest know.   *John 16:22*
I spent long years for thee;   *John 1:10, 11*
Hast thou spent one for Me?   *I Pet. 4:2*

My Father's home of light,   *John 17:5*
    My rainbow-circled throne,   *Rev. 4:3*
I left, for earthly night,   *Phil. 2:7*
    For wanderings sad and lone.   *Matt. 7:20*
I left it all for thee;   *II Cor. 8:9*
Hast thou left aught for Me?   *Luke 10:29*

I suffered much for thee,   *Isa. 53:5*
    More than thy tongue may tell.   *Matt. 26:39*
Of bitterest agony,   *Luke 22:44*
    To rescue thee from hell.   *Rom 5:9*
I suffered much for thee;   *I Pet. 2:21-24*
What canst thou bear for Me?   *Rom. 8:17, 18*

And I have brought to thee,	*John 4:10, 14*
Down from My home above,	*John 3:13*
Salvation full and free,	*Rev. 21:6*
My pardon and My love.	*Acts 5:31*
Great gifts I brought to thee;	*Ps. 68:18*
What hast thou brought to Me?	*Rom. 12:1*
Oh, let thy life be given,	*Rom. 6:13*
Thy years for Me be spent,	*II Cor. 5:15*
World-fetters all be riven,	*Phil. 3:8*
And joy with suffering blent.	*I Pet. 4:13-16*
I gave Myself for thee;	*Eph. 5:2*
Give thou thyself to Me!	*Prov. 23:26*

THE MINISTRY OF SONG

THE ONE REALITY

FOG-WREATHS of doubt in blinding eddies drifted,
    Whirlwinds of fancy, countergusts of thought,
    Shadowless shadows where warm lives were sought,
Numb feet, that feel not their own tread uplifted
On clouds of formless wonder, lightning-rifted!
    What marvel that the whole world's life should seem,
    To helpless intellect, a Brahma-dream,
From which the real and restful is out-sifted!
    Through the dim storm a white peace-bearing Dove
Gleams, and the mist rolls back, the shadows flee,
    The dream is past. A clear calm sky above,
Firm rock beneath; a royal-scrolled tree,
    And One, thorn-diademed, the King of Love
The Son of God, who gave Himself for me!

UNDER THE SURFACE

ACCEPTED

Accepted in the Beloved.　Ephesians 1:6
Perfect in Christ Jesus.　Colossians 1:28
Complete in Him.　Colossians 2:10

ACCEPTED, Perfect and Complete,
For God's inheritance made meet!
How true, how glorious, and how sweet!

In the Beloved — by the King
Accepted, though not anything
But forfeit lives had we to bring.

And Perfect in Christ Jesus made,
On Him our great transgressions laid
We in His righteousness arrayed.

Complete in Him, our glorious Head,
With Jesus raised from the dead,
And by His mighty Spirit led!

O blessed Lord, is this for me?
Then let my whole life henceforth be
One Alleluia-song to Thee!

UNDER THE SURFACE

JUSTIFIED

*This is the name wherewith
she shall be called, The
Lord our Righteousness.*
Jeremiah 33:16

ISRAEL of God, awaken! Church of Christ, arise and shine!
Mourning garb and soiled raiment henceforth be no longer thine!
For the Lord thy God hath clothed thee with a new and glorious
    dress,
With the garments of salvation, with the robe of righteousness.

By the grace of God the Father thou art freely justified,
Through the great redemption purchased by the blood of Him who
    died;
By His Life, for thee fulfilling God's command exceeding broad,
By His glorious resurrection, seal and signet of thy God.

Therefore, justified for ever by the faith which He hath given,
Peace, and joy, and hope abounding, smooth thy trial path to
    heaven:
Unto Him betrothed for ever, who thy life shall crown and bless,
By His name thou shalt be called, Christ, "The Lord our
    Righteousness!"

UNDER THE SURFACE

SANCTIFIED

Sanctified in Christ Jesus.
I Corinthians 1:2

CHURCH of God, beloved and chosen, Church of Christ, for whom
    He died,
Claim thy gifts and praise thy Giver! — *"Ye are washed and
    sanctified."*
Sanctified by God the Father, and by Jesus Christ His Son,
And by God the Holy Spirit, Holy, Holy Three in One.

By His will He sanctifieth, by the Spirit's power within;
By the loving Hand that chasteneth fruits of righteousness to win;
By His truth and by His promise, by the Word, His gift unpriced;
By His own blood, and by union with the risen life of Christ.

Holiness by faith in Jesus, not by effort of thine own, —
Sin's dominion crushed and broken by the power of grace alone, —
God's own holiness within thee, His own beauty on thy brow, —
This shall be thy pilgrim brightness, this thy blessed portion now.

He will sanctify thee wholly; body, spirit, soul shall be
Blameless till thy Saviour's coming in His glorious majesty!
He hath perfected for ever those whom He hath sanctified;
Spotless, glorious, and holy is the Church, His chosen Bride!

UNDER THE SURFACE

I KNOW

I know the crimson stain of sin,
Defiling all without, within;
But now rejoicingly I know
That He has washed me white as snow.
I praise Him for the cleansing tide,
Because I know that Jesus died.

I know the sorrow that is known,
To the tear-burdened heart alone;
But now I know its full relief
Through Him who was acquaint with grief,
And peace through every trial flows,
Because I know that Jesus knows.

I know the shrinking and the fear.
When all seems wrong, and nothing clear;
But now I gaze upon His throne,
And faith sees all His foes o'erthrown,
And I can wait till He explains,
Because I know that Jesus reigns.

THREEFOLD PRAISE

I COULD NOT DO WITHOUT THEE

I could not do without Thee,
    O Saviour of the lost!
Whose precious blood redeemed me,
    At such tremendous cost.
Thy righteousness, Thy pardon,
    Thy precious blood must be
My only hope and comfort,
    My glory and my plea!

I could not do without Thee!
    I cannot stand alone,
I have no strength or goodness,
    No wisdom of my own.
But Thou, beloved Saviour,
    Art all in all to me;
And weakness will be power,
    If leaning hard on Thee.

I could not do without Thee!
    For oh! the way is long,
And I am often weary,
    And sigh replaces song.
How could I do without Thee?
    I do not know the way;
Thou knowest and Thou leadest,
    And wilt not let me stray.

I could not do without Thee,
    O Jesus, Saviour dear!
E'en when my eyes are holden,
    I know that Thou art near,
How dreary and how lonely
    This changeful life would be
Without the sweet communion,
    The secret rest with Thee!

I could not do without Thee!
    No other friend can read
The spirit's strange deep longings,
    Interpreting its need.
No human heart could enter
    Each dim recess of mine,
And soothe and hush and calm it,
    O blessed Lord, but Thine!

I could not do without Thee!
    For years are fleeting fast,
And soon, in solemn loneliness,
    The river must be passed.
But Thou wilt never leave me,
    And, though the waves roll high,
I know Thou wilt be near me,
    And whisper, "It is I."

UNDER THE SURFACE

CHILDREN

And Jesus called a little

child unto him, and set

him in the midst of them.

MATTHEW 18:2

THY KINGDOM COME

GOD of heaven! hear our singing;
  Only little ones are we,
Yet a great petition bringing,
  Father, now we come to Thee.

Let Thy kingdom come, we pray Thee,
  Let the world in Thee find rest;
Let all know Thee, and obey Thee,
  Loving, praising, blessing, blessed!

Let the sweet and joyful story
  Of the Saviour's wondrous love,
Wake on earth a song of glory,
  Like the angel's song above.

Father, send the glorious hour,
  Every heart be Thine alone!
For the kingdom, and the power,
  And the glory are Thine own.

CHORDS FOR CH!LDREN

EVENING PRAYER

NOW the light has gone away,
Saviour, listen while I pray,
Asking Thee to watch and keep,
And to send me quiet sleep.

Jesus, Saviour, wash away
All that has been wrong today,
Help me every day to be
Good and gentle, more like Thee.

Let my near and dear ones be
Always near and dear to Thee;
Oh, bring me and all I love
To Thy happy home above.

Now my evening praise I give;
Thou didst die that I might live,
All my blessings come from Thee;
Oh, how good Thou art to me!

Thou, my blest and kindest Friend,
Thou wilt love me to the end!
Let me love Thee more and more.
Always better than before!

CHORDS FOR CHILDREN

THE MOON

The moon walking in brightness.
Job 31:26

NOT long ago the moon was dark,
    No light she gave or gained;
She did not look upon the sun,
    So all her glory waned.
Now through the sky so broad and high,
    In robe of shining whiteness,
Among the solemn stars of God,
    She walks in brightness.

Look up to Him who is the Sun,
    The True and Only Light,
And seek the glory of His face,
    His smile so dear and bright.
Then making gladness all around,
    By gentleness and rightness,
You, too, shall shine with light divine,
    And walk in brightness.

CHORDS FOR CHILDREN

JESSIE'S FRIEND

LITTLE Jessie, darling pet,
　　Do you want a friend?
One who never will forget,
　　Loving to the end;
One whom you can tell when sad
　　Everything that grieves;
One who loves to make you glad,
　　One who never leaves.

Such a loving Friend is ours,
　　Near us all the day,
Helping us in lesson hours,
　　Smiling on our play;
Keeping us from doing wrong,
　　Guarding everywhere,
Listening to each happy song
　　And each little prayer.

Jessie, if you only knew
　　What He is to me,
Surely you would seek Him too,
　　You would "come and see."
Come, and you will find it true,
　　Happy you will be;
Jesus says, and says to you,
　　"Come, oh come to Me."

CHORDS FOR CHILDREN

WHO WILL TAKE CARE OF ME?

WHO will take care of me? darling, you say!
　　Lovingly, tenderly watched as you are!
Listen! I give you the answer today,
　　ONE who is never forgetful or far!

He will take care of you! all through the day,
　　Jesus is near you to keep you from ill;
Walking or resting, at lessons or play,
　　Jesus is with you and watching you still.

He will take care of you! all through the night,
　　Jesus, the Shepherd, His little one keeps;
Darkness to Him is the same as the light;
　　He never slumbers and He never sleeps.

He will take care of you! all through the year,
　　Crowning each day with His kindness and love,
Sending you blessing and shielding from fear,
　　Leading you on to the bright home above.

He will take care of you! yes, to the end!
　　Nothing can alter His love to His own.
Darling, be glad that you have such a Friend,
　　He will not leave you one moment alone!

CHORDS FOR CHILDREN

HAVE you not a song for Jesus?
　　All the little buds and flowers,
All the merry birds and breezes,
　　All the sunbeams and the showers,
Praise Him in their own sweet way!
What have you to sing today?
Bring your happiest songs, and sing
For your Saviour and your King.

CHORDS FOR CHILDREN

NEW YEAR HYMN

JESUS, blessed Saviour,
 Help us now to raise
Songs of glad thanksgiving,
 Songs of holy praise.
O how kind and gracious
 Thou hast always been!
O how many blessings
 Every day hast seen!
  Jesus, blessed Saviour,
   Now our praises hear,
  For Thy grace and favour
   Crowning all the year.

Jesus, holy Saviour,
 Only Thou canst tell
How we often stumbled,
 How we often fell!
All our sins (so many),
 Saviour, Thou dost know;
In Thy blood most precious,
 Wash us white as snow.
  Jesus, blessed Saviour,
   Keep us in Thy fear,
  Let Thy grace and favour
   Pardon all the year.

Jesus, loving Saviour,
    Only Thou dost know
All that may befall us
    As we onward go.
So we humbly pray Thee,
    Take us by the hand,
Lead us ever upward
    To the Better Land.
      Jesus, blessed Saviour,
        Keep us ever near,
        Let Thy grace and favour
        Shield us all the year.

CHORDS FOR CHILDREN

THE CHILDREN'S TRIUMPH

THE Sunbeams came to my window,
  And said, "Come out and see
The sparkle on the river,
  The blossom on the tree!"
But never a moment parleyed I
  With the bright-haired Sunbeams' call!
Though their dazzling hands on the leaf they laid,
I drew it away to the curtain-shade,
  Where a sunbeam could not fall.

The Robins came to my window,
  And said, "Come out and sing!
Come out and join the chorus
  Of the festival of Spring!"
But never a carol would I trill
  In the festival of May;
But I sat alone in my shadowy room
And worked away in its quiet gloom,
  And the Robins flew away.

The Children came to my window,
  And said, "Come out and play!
Come out with us in the sunshine,
  'Tis such a glorious day!"
Then never another word I wrote,
  And my desk was put away!
When the Children called me, what could I do?
The Robins might fail, and the Sunbeams too,
  But the children won the day.

UNDER THE SURFACE

NEEDS
AND
CONSOLATION

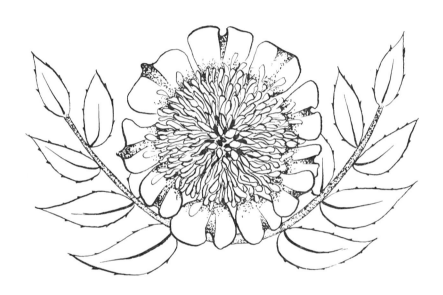

Be careful for nothing;

but in every thing by prayer

and supplication with

thanksgiving let your requests

be made known unto God.

PHILIPPIANS 4:6

GOD THE PROVIDER

WHO shall tell our untold need,
　　Deeply felt, though scarcely known?
Who the hungering soul can feed,
　　Guard, and guide, but God alone?
Blessed promise! while we see
Earthly friends must powerless be,
Earthly fountains quickly dry,
"God" shall all your need supply.

He hath said it! so we know
　　Nothing less can we receive.
Oh that thankful love may glow
　　While we restfully believe, —
Ask not how, but trust Him still;
Ask not when, but wait His will:
Simply on His word rely,
God *"shall"* all your need supply.

Through the whole of life's long way,
　　Outward, inward need we trace;
Need arising day by day,
　　Patience, wisdom, strength, and grace.
Needing Jesus most of all,
Full of need, on Him we call;
Then how gracious His reply,
God shall *"all"* your need supply.

Great our need, but greater far
    Is our Father's loving power;
He upholds each mighty star,
    He unfolds each tiny flower.
He who numbers every hair,
Earnest of His faithful care,
Gave His Son for us to die:
God shall all *"your"* need supply.

Yet we often vainly plead
    For a fancied good denied,
What we deemed a pressing need
    Still remaining unsupplied.
Yet from dangers all concealed,
Thus our wisest Friend doth shield;
No *good* thing will He deny,
God shall all your *"need"* supply.

Can we count redemption's treasure,
    Scan the glory of God's love?
Such shall be the boundless measure
    Of His blessings from above.
All we ask or think, and more,
He will give in bounteous store;
He can fill and satisfy,
God shall all your need *"supply."*

One the channel, deep and broad,
    From the Fountain of the Throne,
Christ the Saviour, Son of God,
    Blessings flow through Him alone.
He, the Faithful and the True,
Brings us mercies ever new:
Till we reach His home on high,
"God shall all your need supply."

THE MINISTRY OF SONG

[138]

FAITH'S QUESTION

TO whom, O Saviour, shall we go
    For life, and joy, and light?
No help, no comfort from below,
No lasting gladness we may know.
    No hope may bless our sight.
Our souls are weary and athirst,
But earth is iron-bound and cursed,
And nothing she may yield can stay
The restless yearnings day by day;
Yet, without Thee, Redeemer blest,
We would not, if we could find rest.

To whom, O Saviour, shall we go?
    We gaze around in vain.
Though pleasure's fairy lute be strung,
And mirth's enchaining lay be sung,
    We dare not trust the strain.
The touch of sorrow or of sin
Hath saddened all, without, within;
What here we fondly love and prize,
However beauteous be its guise,
Has passed, is passing, or may pass,
Like frost-fringe on the autumn grass.

To whom, O Saviour, shall we go?
    Our spirits dimly wait,
Imprisoned in our mortal frame,

And only one of direful name
    Can force its sin-barred gate.
Our loved ones can but greet us through
The dungeon grate, from which we view
All outward things. They enter not:
Thou, Thou alone canst cheer our lot.
O Christ, we long for Thee to dwell
Within our solitary cell!

To whom, O Saviour, shall we go?
    Unless Thy voice we hear,
All tuneless falls the sweetest song,
And lonely seems the busiest throng
    Unless we feel Thee near.
We dare not think what earth would be,
Thou Heaven-Creator, but for Thee;
A howling chaos, wild and dark —
One flood of horror, while no ark,
Upborne above the gloom-piled wave,
From one great death-abyss might save.

To whom, O Saviour, shall we go?
    The Tempter's power is great;
E'en in our hearts is evil bound,
And, lurking stealthily around,
    Still for our souls doth wait.
Thou tempted One, whose suffering heart
In all our sorrows bore a part,
Whose life-blood only could atone,
Too weak are we to stand alone;
And nothing but Thy shield of light
Can guard us in the dreaded fight.

To whom, O Saviour, shall we go?
    The night of death draws near;
Its shadow must be passed alone,
No friend can with our souls go down,
    The untried way to cheer.

Thou hast the words of endless life;
Thou givest victory in the strife;
Thou only art the changeless Friend,
On whom for aye we may depend:
In life, in death, alike we flee,
O Saviour of the world, to THEE.

THE MINISTRY OF SONG

GROWING

UNTO him that hath, Thou givest
 Ever "more abundantly."
Lord, I live because Thou livest,
 Therefore give more life to me;
Therefore speed me in the race;
 Therefore let me grow in grace.

Deepen all Thy work, O Master,
 Strengthen every downward root,
Only do Thou ripen faster,
 More and more, Thy pleasant fruit.
Purge me, prune me, self abase,
 Only let me grow in grace.

Jesus, grace for grace outpouring,
 Show me ever greater things;
Raise me higher, sunward soaring,
 Mounting as on eagle-wings.
By the brightness of Thy face,
 Jesus, let me grow in grace.

Let me grow by sun and shower,
 Every moment water me;
Make me really hour by hour
 More and more conformed to Thee,

That Thy loving eye may trace,
Day by day, my growth in grace.

Let me then be always growing,
    Never, never standing still;
Listening, learning, better knowing
    Thee and Thy most blessed will.
Till I reach Thy holy place,
Daily let me grow in grace.

LOYAL RESPONSES

INCREASE OUR FAITH

INCREASE our faith, beloved Lord!
    For Thou alone canst give
The faith that takes Thee at Thy word,
    The faith by which we live.

Increase our faith! So weak are we,
    That we both may and must
Commit our very faith to Thee,
    Entrust to Thee our trust.

Increase our faith! for there is yet
    Much land to be possessed;
And by no other strength we get
    Our heritage to rest.

Increase our faith! On this broad shield
    "All" fiery darts be caught;
We must be victors in the field
    Where Thou for us hast fought.

Increase our faith, that we may claim
    Each starry promise sure,
And *always* triumph in Thy name,
    And to the end endure.

Increase our faith, O Lord, we pray,
    That we may not depart
From Thy commands, but *all* obey
    With free and loyal heart.

Increase our faith — increase it still —
    From heavenward hour to hour,
And in us gloriously "fulfil
    The work of faith with power."

Increase our faith, that never dim
    Or trembling it may be,
Crowned with the "perfect peace" of him
    "Whose mind is stayed on Thee."

Increase our faith, for Thou hast prayed
    That it should never fail;
Our stedfast anchorage is made
    With Thee, within the veil.

Increase our faith, that unto Thee
    More fruit may still abound;
That it may grow "exceedingly,"
    And to Thy praise be found.

Increase our faith, O Saviour dear,
    By Thy sweet sovereign grace,
Till, changing faith for vision clear,
    We see Thee face to face!

LOYAL RESPONSES

THE RIGHT WAY

LORD, is it still the right way, though I cannot see Thy face,
Though I do not feel Thy presence and Thine all-sustaining grace?
Can even this be leading through the bleak and sunless wild
To the City of Thy holy rest, the mansions undefiled?

Lord, is it still the right way? A while ago I passed
Where every step seemed thornier and harder than the last;
Where bitterest disappointment and inly aching sorrow
Carved day by day a weary cross, renewed with every morrow.

The heaviest end of that strange cross I knew was laid on Thee;
So I could still press on, secure of Thy deep sympathy.
Our upward path may well be steep, else how were patience tried?
I knew it was the right way, for it led me to Thy side.

But now I wait alone amid dim shadows dank and chill;
All moves and changes round me, but I seem standing still;
Or every feeble footstep I urge towards the light
Seems but to lead me farther into the silent night.

I cannot hear Thy voice, Lord! dost Thou still hear my cry?
I cling to Thine assurance that Thou art ever nigh;
I know that Thou art faithful; I trust, but cannot see,
That it is still the right way by which Thou leadest me.

I think I could go forward with brave and joyful heart,
Though every step should pierce me with unknown fiery smart.

If only I might see Thee, if I might gaze above
On all the cloudless glory of the sunshine of Thy love.

Is it really leading onwards? When the shadows flee away,
Shall I find this path has brought me more near to perfect day?
Or am I left to wander thus that I may stretch my hand
To some still wearier traveller in this same shadow-land?

Is this Thy chosen training for some future task unknown?
Is it that I may learn to rest upon Thy word alone?
Whate'er it be, oh! leave me not, fulfil Thou every hour
The purpose of Thy goodness, and the work of faith with power.

I lay my prayer before Thee, and, trusting in Thy word,
Though all is silence in my heart, I know that Thou hast heard.
To that blest City lead me, Lord (still choosing all my way),
Where faith melts into vision as the starlight into day.

THE MINISTRY OF SONG

MASTER, SAY ON!

MASTER, speak! Thy servant heareth,
    Waiting for Thy gracious word,
Longing for Thy voice that cheereth;
    Master! let it now be heard.
I am listening, Lord, for Thee;
What hast Thou to say to me?

Master, speak in love and power:
    Crown the mercies of the day,
In this quiet evening hour
    Of the moonrise o'er the bay,
With the music of Thy voice;
Speak! and bid Thy child rejoice.

Often through my heart is pealing
    Many another voice than Thine,
Many an unwilled echo stealing
    From the walls of this Thy shrine:
Let Thy longed-for accents fall;
Master, speak! and silence all.

Master, speak! I do not doubt Thee,
    Though so tearfully I plead;

Saviour, Shepherd! oh, without Thee
    Life would be a blank indeed!
But I long for fuller light,
Deeper love and clearer sight.

Resting on the "faithful saying,"
    Trusting what Thy Gospel saith,
On Thy written promise staying
    All my hope in life and death,
Yet I long for something more
From Thy love's exhaustless store.

Speak to me by name, O Master,
    Let me know it is to me;
Speak, that I may follow faster,
    With a step more firm and free,
Where the Shepherd leads the flock,
In the shadow of the Rock.

Master, speak! I kneel before Thee,
    Listening, longing, waiting still;
Oh, how long shall I implore Thee
    This petition to fulfil?
Hast Thou not one word for me?
Must my prayer unanswered be?

Master, speak! though least and lowest,
    Let me not unheard depart;
Master, speak! for oh, Thou knowest
    All the yearning of my heart,
Knowest all its truest need;
Speak! and make me blest indeed.

Master, speak! and make me ready,
    When Thy voice is truly heard,

With obedience glad and steady
Still to follow every word.
I am listening, Lord, for Thee;
Master, speak, oh, speak to me!

THE MINISTRY OF SONG

COMPENSATION

OH, the compensating springs! Oh, the balance-wheels of life,
Hidden away in the workings under the seeming strife!
Slowing the fret and the friction, weighting the whirl and the force,
Evolving the truest power from each unconscious source.

How shall we gauge the whole, who can only guess a part?
How can we read the life, when we cannot spell the heart?
How shall we measure another, we who can never know
From the juttings above the surface the depth of the vein below?

Even our present way is known to ourselves alone,
Height and abyss and torrent, flower and thorn and stone;
But we gaze on another's path as a far-off mountain scene,
Scanning the outlined hills, but never the vales between.

How shall we judge their present, we who have never seen
That which is past for ever, and that which might have been?
Measuring by ourselves, unwise indeed we are,
Measuring what we know by what we can hardly see.

Ah! if we knew it all, we should surely understand
That the balance of sorrow and joy is held with an even hand;
That the scale of success or loss shall never overflow,
And that compensation is twined with the lot of high and low.

The easy path in the lowland hath little grand or new,
But a toilsome ascent leads on to a wide and glorious view;

Peopled and warm is the valley, lonely and chill the height,
But the peak that is nearer the storm-cloud is nearer the stars of
      light.

Launch on the foaming stream that bears you along like a dart, —
There is danger of rapid and rock, there is tension of muscle and
      heart;
Glide on the easy current, monotonous, calm, and slow,
You are spared the quiver and strain in the safe and quiet flow.

Oh, the sweetness that dwells in a harp of many strings,
While each, all vocal with love, in tuneful harmony rings!
But oh, the wail and the discord, when one and another is rent,
Tensionless, broken, or lost, from the cherished instrument.

For rapture of love is linked with the pain or fear of loss,
And the hand that takes the crown must ache with many a cross;
Yet he who hath never a conflict hath never a victor's palm,
And only the toilers know the sweetness of rest and calm.

Only between the storms can the Alpine traveller know
Transcendent glory of clearness, marvels of gleam and glow;
Had he the brightness unbroken of cloudless summer days,
This had been dimmed by the dust and the veil of a brooding haze.

Who would dare the choice, neither or both to know,
The finest quiver of joy or the agony-thrill of woe?
Never the exquisite pain, then never the exquisite bliss,
For the heart that is dull to that can never be strung to this.

Great is the peril or toil if the glory or gain be great;
Never an earthly gift without responsible weight;
Never a treasure without a following shade of care;
Never a power without the lurk of a subtle snare.

For the swift is not the safe, and the sweet is not the strong,
The smooth is not the short, and the keen is not the long;

The much is not the most, and the wide is not the deep,
And the flow is never a spring, when the ebb is only neap.

Then hush! oh, hush! for the Father knows what thou knowest not,
The need and the thorn and the shadow linked with the fairest lot;
Knows the wisest exemption from many an unseen snare,
Knows what will keep thee nearest, knows what thou couldst not
      bear.

Hush! oh, hush! for the Father portioneth as He will
To all His beloved children, and shall they not be still?
Is not His will the wisest, is not His choice the best?
And in perfect acquiescence is there not perfect rest?

Hush! oh, hush! for the Father, whose ways are true and just,
Knoweth and careth and loveth, and waits for thy perfect trust;
The cup He is slowly filling shall soon be full to the brim,
And infinite compensations for ever be found in Him.

Hush! oh, hush! for the Father hath fulness of joy in store,
Treasures of power and wisdom, and pleasures for evermore;
Blessing and honour and glory, endless, infinite bliss; —
Child of His love and His choice, oh, canst thou not wait for this?

UNDER THE SURFACE

FRESH SPRINGS

*All my fresh springs shall
be in Thee.* Psalm 87:7

HEAR the Father's ancient promise!
    Listen, thirsty, weary one!
"I will pour My Holy Spirit
    On Thy chosen seed, O Son."
Promise to the Lord's Anointed,
    Gift of God to Him for thee!
Now, by covenant appointed,
    All thy springs in Him shall be.

Springs of life in desert places
    Shall thy God unseal for thee;
Quickening and reviving graces,
    Dew-like, healing, sweet, and free.
Springs of sweet refreshment flowing,
    When thy work is hard or long,
Courage, hope, and power bestowing,
    Lightening labour with a song.

Springs of peace, when conflict heightens
    Thine uplifted eye shall see;
Peace that strengthens, calms, and brightens,
    Peace itself a victory.
Springs of comfort, strangely springing
    Through the bitter wells of woe;
Founts of hidden gladness, bringing
    Joy that earth can ne'er bestow.

Thine, O Christian, is this treasure,
    To thy risen Head assured!
Thine in full and gracious measure,
    Thine by covenant secured!
Now arise! His word possessing,
    Claim the promise of the Lord;
Plead through Christ for showers of blessing,
    Till the Spirit be outpoured!

UNDER THE SURFACE

NOW AND AFTERWARD

NOW, the sowing and the weeping,
  Working hard and waiting long;
Afterward, the golden reaping,
  Harvest-home and grateful song.

Now, the pruning, sharp, unsparing,
  Scattered blossom, bleeding shoot!
Afterward, the plenteous bearing
  Of the Master's pleasant fruit.

Now, the plunge, the briny burden,
  Blind, faint gropings in the sea;
Afterward, the pearly guerdon
  That shall make the diver free.

Now, the long and toilsome duty
  Stone by stone to carve and bring;
Afterward, the perfect beauty
  Of the palace of the King.

Now, the tuning and the tension,
  Wailing minors, discord strong;
Afterward, the grand ascension
  Of the Alleluia song.

Now, the spirit conflict-riven,
  Wounded heart, unequal strife;

Afterward, the triumph given,
    And the victor's crown of life.

Now, the training, strange and lowly,
    Unexplained and tedious now;
Afterward, the service holy,
    And the Master's "Enter thou!"

UNDER THE SURFACE

NOT FORSAKEN

OH, not forsaken! God gives better things
    Than thou hast asked in thy forlornest hour.
    Love's promises shall be fulfilled in power.
Not death, but life; not silence, but the strings
Of angel-harps; no deep, cold sea, but springs
    Of living water; no dim, wearied sight,
    Nor time- nor tear-mist, but the joy of light;
Not sleep, but rest that happy service brings;
And no forgotten name thy lot shall be,
    But God's remembrance. Thou canst never drift
        Beyond His love. Would I could reach thee where
    The shadows droop so heavily, and lift
        The cold weight from thy life — And if I care
For one unknown, oh, how much more doth HE!

UNDER THE SURFACE

PEACEABLE FRUIT

*Nevertheless, afterward
it yieldeth the peaceable
fruit of righteousness.*
Hebrews 12:11

WHAT shall Thine "afterward" be, O Lord,
    For this dark and suffering night?
Father, what shall Thine "afterward" be?
Hast Thou a morning of joy for me,
    And a new and joyous light?
What shall Thine "afterward" be, O Lord,
    For the moan that I cannot stay?
Shall it issue in some new song of praise,
Sweeter than sorrowless heart could raise,
    When the night hath passed away?

What shall Thine "afterward" be, O Lord,
    For this helplessness of pain?
A clearer view of my home above,
Of my Father's strength and my Father's love?
    Shall this be my lasting gain?
What shall Thine "afterward" be, O Lord?
    How long must Thy child endure?
Thou knowest! 'Tis well that I know it not!
Thine "afterward" cometh, I cannot tell what,
    But I know that Thy word is sure.
What shall Thine "afterward" be, O Lord?
    I wonder and wait to see
(While to Thy chastening Hand I bow)
What "peaceable fruit" may be ripening now,
    Ripening fast for Thee!

UNDER THE SURFACE

[159]

I LEAVE IT ALL WITH THEE

YES, I will leave it all with Thee,
And only ask that I may be
Submissive to Thy loving will,
Confiding, waiting, trusting still.
Thou every fond desire dost know
Which in my inmost heart doth glow;
Thou hearest every secret sigh
When silent sorrow's power is nigh.
Omniscience alone may tell
The thoughts which in my spirit dwell;
But 'tis a soothing word to me,
"My Father every thought can see."
He knows them all — the hopes — the fears —
Confided not to mortal ears.
He knows the deep intensity
Of feelings wakened now in me.
And if He knows then, 'tis enough!
I need not fear a stern rebuff;
There's sympathy within His breast,
On which my weary heart can rest.
Nor is there sympathy alone,
Almighty is my Father's throne,
And He can grant me each desire;
His gracious hand may never tire.
He *can*. But *will* He? Trust Him yet,
My faithless soul! Can I forget

That He hath passed His word of old, —
"Not one good thing will He withhold
From them, the children of my love,
Whose hearts are set on things above"?
Not one good thing! But can I see
What may be good, what ill for me?
Can I unbar the massy gate
Which hides from me the way I take?
But His eye turneth night to day,
E'en like the lightning's piercing ray;
Then here is my security,
That God my truest good doth see.
That joy which earnestly I crave,
O'er which my fondest hopes now wave,
Might prove to me the shade of death!
That healing breeze — the Simoom's breath,
If so — it never will be mine.
At such a loss shall I repine?
No! let me rather praise the Hand
Which looseneth the dangerous band.
But if it be a heaven-born plant,
For whose sweet flowers my soul doth pant,
If heavenly gladness it shall bring,
And raise my soul on angel wing,
Till nearer Thee each day I live, —
Oh, then that blessing Thou wilt give.
The joy scarce hoped for shall be mine,
A deeply grateful heart be Thine!
Then I will leave it all with Thee!
My Father, grant that I may be
Submissive to Thine own good will,
Confiding, waiting, loving still!

EARLY POEMS

HOLY DAYS
AND
SPECIAL
OCCASIONS

This is the day which the

Lord hath made; we will

rejoice and be glad in it.

PSALM 118:24

ADVENT SONG

THOU art coming, O my Saviour!
    Thou art coming, O my King!
In Thy beauty all-resplendent,
In Thy glory all-transcendent;
    Well may we rejoice and sing!
Coming! in the opening east,
    Herald brightness slowly swells;
Coming! O my glorious Priest,
    Hear we not Thy golden bells?

Thou art coming, Thou art coming!
    We shall meet Thee on Thy way,
We shall see Thee, we shall know Thee,
We shall bless Thee, we shall show Thee
    All our hearts could never say!
What an anthem that will be,
Ringing out our love to Thee,
Pouring out our rapture sweet
At Thine own all-glorious feet!

Thou art coming! Rays of glory,
    Through the veil Thy death has rent,
Touch the mountain and the river
With a golden glowing quiver,
    Thrill of light and music blent.
Earth is brightened when this gleam
Falls on flower and rock and stream;
Life is brightened when this ray
Falls upon its darkest day.

Not a cloud and not a shadow,
    Not a mist and not a tear,

Not a sin and not a sorrow,
Not a dim and veiled tomorrow,
    For that sunrise grand and clear!
Jesus, Saviour, once with Thee,
    Nothing else seems worth a thought!
Oh, how marvellous will be
    All the bliss Thy pain hath bought!

Thou art coming! At Thy table
    We are witnesses for this,
While remembering hearts Thou meetest,
In communion clearest, sweetest,
Earnest of our coming bliss.
Showing not Thy death alone,
    And Thy love exceeding great,
But Thy coming and Thy throne,
    All for which we long and wait.

Thou art coming! We are waiting
    With a hope that cannot fail;
Asking not the day or hour,
Resting on Thy word of power,
    Anchored safe within the veil.
Time appointed may be long,
    But the vision must be sure:
Certainty shall make us strong,
    Joyful patience can endure!

Oh the joy to see Thee reigning,
    Thee, my own beloved Lord!
Every tongue Thy name confessing,
Worship, honour, glory, blessing,
    Brought to Thee with glad accord!
Thee, my Master and my Friend,
    Vindicated and enthroned!
Unto earth's remotest end
    Glorified, adored, and owned!

UNDER THE SURFACE

CHRISTMAS SUNSHINE

DO the angels know the blessed day,
    And strike their harps anew?
Then may the echo of their lay
    Float sweetly down to you,
And fill your soul with Christmas song
That your heart shall echo your whole life long.

JESUS came! — and came for me.
    Simple words! and yet expressing
Depths of holy mystery,
    Depths of wondrous love and blessing.
Holy Spirit, make me see
All His coming means for me;
Take the things of Christ, I pray,
Show them to my heart today.

THERE is silence high in the midnight sky,
    And only the sufferers watch the night,
But long ago there was song and glow,
    And a message of joy from the Prince of Light,
And the Christmas song of the messenger-throng
The echoes of life shall for ever prolong.

CHRIST is come to be my Friend,
    Leading loving to the end!
Christ is come to be my King,
Ordering, ruling everything.
Christ is come! enough for me,
Lonely though the pathway be.

GIVE me a song, O Lord,
    That I may sing to Thee,
In true and sweet accord,
    With angel minstrelsy.
Oh tune my heart that it may bring
A Christmas anthem to my King!

CLOSING CHORDS

A MERRIE CHRISTMAS

"A merrie Christmas" to you!
    For we serve the Lord with mirth,
And we carol forth glad tidings
    Of our holy Saviour's birth.
So we keep the olden greeting
    With its meaning deep and true,
And wish "a merrie Christmas"
    And a happy New Year to you!

Oh, yes! "a merrie Christmas,"
    With lithest song and smile,
Bright with the thought of Him who dwelt
    On earth a little while,
That we might dwell for ever
    Where never falls a tear:
So "a merrie Christmas" to you,
    And a happy, happy year!

MISCELLANEOUS

LOVE AND LIGHT FOR THE NEW YEAR

"NOT as the world giveth
      Give I to you!"
Saith the Redeemer,
      Faithful and true.
May He enrich thee,
      This New Year's Day,
With gifts from His treasure
      That pass not away.

THIS New Year Thou givest me,
            Lord, I consecrate to Thee,
      With all its nights and days;
Fill my hand with service blest,
Fill my heart with holy rest,
      And fill my life with praise.

ANOTHER year for Jesus!
      How can I wish for you
A greater joy or blessing,
      A fellow-worker true?
Eternity with Jesus
      Is long enough for rest;
Thank God that we are spared to work
      For Him whom we love best!

IS the work difficult?
  Jesus directs thee.
Is the path dangerous?
  Jesus protects thee.
Fear not, and falter not;
  Let the word cheer thee!
All through the coming year
  He will be with thee!

CLOSING CHORDS

A HAPPY NEW YEAR TO YOU

NEW mercies, new blessings, new light on thy way;
New courage, new hope, and new strength for each day;
New notes of thanksgiving, new chords of delight,
New praise in the morning, new songs in the night;
New wine in thy chalice, new altars to raise;
New fruits for thy Master, new garments of praise;
New gifts from His treasures, new smiles from His face;
New streams from the fountain of infinite grace;
New stars for thy crown, and new tokens of love;
New gleams of the glory that waits thee above;
New light of His countenance full and unpriced; —
All this be the joy of thy new life in Christ!

MISCELLANEOUS

ANOTHER YEAR

ANOTHER year is dawning!
　　Dear Master, let it be,
In working or in waiting,
　　Another year with Thee.

Another year of leaning
　　Upon Thy loving breast,
Of ever-deepening trustfulness,
　　Of quiet, happy rest.

Another year of mercies,
　　Of faithfulness and grace;
Another year of gladness
　　In the shining of Thy face.

Another year of progress,
　　Another year of praise;
Another year of proving
　　Thy presence "all the days."

Another year of service,
　　Of witness for Thy love;
Another year of training
　　For holier work above.

Another year is dawning,
　　Dear Master, let it be,
On earth, or else in heaven,
　　Another year for Thee!

MISCELLANEOUS

FAITHFUL PROMISES

STANDING at the portal
   Of the opening year,
Words of comfort meet us,
   Hushing every fear;
Spoken through the silence
   By our Father's voice,
Tender, strong, and faithful,
   Making us rejoice.
      Onward then, and fear not,
        Children of the day,
      For His word shall never,
        Never pass away.

I, the Lord, am with thee,
   Be thou not afraid!
I will help and strengthen,
   Be thou not dismayed!
Yea, I will uphold thee
   With my own right hand;
Thou are called and chosen
   In my sight to stand.
      Onward then, and fear not,
        Children of the day!
      For His word shall never,
        Never pass away!

For the year before us,
   Oh what rich supplies!

For the poor and needy
    Living streams shall rise;
For the sad and sinful
    Shall His grace abound;
For the faint and feeble
    Perfect strength be found.
        Onward then, and fear not,
        Children of the day!
        For His word shall never,
        Never pass away!

He will never fail us,
    He will not forsake;
His eternal covenant
    He will never break!
Resting on His promise,
    What have we to fear?
God is all-sufficient
    For the coming year.
        Onward then, and fear not,
        Children of the day!
        For His word shall never,
        Never pass away!

MISCELLANEOUS

AN EASTER PRAYER

OH let me know
The power of Thy resurrection;
   Oh let me show
Thy risen life in calm and clear reflection;
   Oh let me soar
Where Thou, my Saviour Christ, art gone before;
   In mind and heart
Let me dwell always, only, where Thou art.

   Oh let me give
Out of the gifts Thou freely givest;
   Oh let me live
With life abundantly because Thou livest;
   Oh make me shine
In darkest places, for Thy light is mine;
   Oh let me be
A faithful witness for Thy truth and Thee.

   Oh let me show
The strong reality of gospel story;
   Oh let me go
From strength to strength, from glory to glory;
   Oh let me sing
For very joy, because Thou art my King;
   Oh let me praise
Thy love and faithfulness through all my days.

CLOSING CHORDS

HE HATH DONE IT!

SING, O heavens! the Lord hath done it!
 Sound it forth o'er land and sea!
Jesus says, "I have redeemed thee,
 Now return, return to Me!"
O return, for His own life-blood
 Paid the ransom, made us free
  Evermore and evermore.

For I know that what He doeth
 Stands for ever, fixed and true;
Nothing can be added to it,
 Nothing left for us to do;
Nothing can be taken from it,
 Done for me and done for you
  Evermore and evermore.

Listen now! the Lord hath done it!
 For He loved us unto death;
It is finished! He has saved us!
 Only trust to what He saith.
He hath done it! Come and bless Him,
 Spend in praise your ransomed breath
  Evermore and evermore.

Oh believe the Lord hath done it!
 Wherefore linger, wherefore doubt?
All the cloud of black transgression
 He Himself hath blotted out.

He hath done it! Come and bless Him,
　　Swell the grand thanksgiving shout
　　Evermore and evermore.

CLOSING CHORDS

ASCENSION SONG

He ascended up on high.
Ephesians 4:8

GOLDEN harps are sounding
Angel voices ring,
Pearly gates are opened —
Opened for the King;
Christ, the King of Glory,
Jesus, King of Love,
Is gone up in triumph
To His throne above.
All His work is ended,
Joyfully we sing,
Jesus hath ascended!
Glory to our King!

He who came to save us,
He who bled and died,
Now is crowned with glory
At His Father's side.
Never more to suffer,
Never more to die:
Jesus, King of Glory,
Is gone up on high.
All His work is ended,
Joyfully we sing!
Jesus hath ascended!
Glory to our King!

Praying for His children
    In that blessed place,
Calling them to glory,
    Sending them His grace;
His bright home preparing,
    Faithful ones, for you;
Jesus ever liveth,
    Ever loveth too.
        All His work is ended,
        Joyfully we sing!
        Jesus hath ascended!
        Glory to our King!

UNDER THE SURFACE

MISCELLANEOUS

Thou wilt show me the path of life . . .

PSALM 16:11

TINY TOKENS

THE murmur of a waterfall
    A mile away,
The rustle when a robin lights
    Upon a spray,
The lapping of a lowland stream
    On dipping boughs,
The sound of grazing from a herd
    Of gentle cows.
The echo from a wooded hill
    Of cuckoo's call,
The quiver through the meadow grass
    At evening fall: —
Too subtle are these harmonies
    For pen and rule,
Such music is not understood
    By any school:
But when the brain is overwrought,
    It hath a spell,
Beyond all human skill and power,
    To make it well.

The memory of a kindly word
    For long gone by,
The fragrance of a fading flower
    Sent lovingly,
The gleaming of a sudden smile
    Or sudden tear,

The warmer pressure of the hand,
  The tone of cheer,
The hush that means "I cannot speak,
  But I have heard!"
The note that only bears a verse
  From God's own Word: —
Such tiny things we hardly count
  As ministry;
The givers deeming they have shown
  Scant sympathy;
But when the heart is overwrought,
  Oh, who can tell
The power of such tiny things
  To make it well!

MISCELLANEOUS

GOLDEN LAND

FAR from home alone I wander
    Over mountain and pathless wave,
But the fair land that shineth yonder
    Claimeth the love that erst it gave.
Golden Land, so far, so nearing!
    Land of those who wait for me!
Ever brighter the vision cheering,
    Golden Land, I haste to thee!

On my path a golden sunlight
    Softly falls where'er I roam,
And I know it is the one light
    Both of exile and of home.
Golden Land, so far, so near,
On my heart engraven clear,
Though I wander from strand to strand,
Dwells my heart in that Golden Land.

MISCELLANEOUS

PERFECT PEACE

LIKE a river glorious
  Is God's perfect peace,
Over all victorious
  In its bright increase.
Perfect — yet it floweth
  Fuller every day;
Perfect — yet it groweth
  Deeper all the way.
Chorus – Stayed upon Jehovah
      Hearts are fully blest.
      Finding as He promised,
      Perfect peace and rest.

Hidden in the hollow
  Of His blessed hand.
Never foe can follow,
  Never traitor stand.
Not a surge of worry,
  Not a shade of care,
Not a blast of hurry
  Touch the spirit there.
Chorus – Stayed upon Jehovah,
      Hearts are fully blest,
      Finding, as He promised,
      Perfect peace and rest.

Every joy or trial
    Falleth from above,
Traced upon our dial
    By the Sun of Love.
We may trust Him solely
    All for us to do;
They who trust Him Wholly,
    Find Him wholly true.
Chorus – Stayed upon Jehovah,
      Hearts are fully blest,
      Finding, as He promised,
      Perfect peace and rest.

LOYAL RESPONSES

EYE HATH NOT SEEN

YOU never write of heaven,
    Though you write of heavenly themes;
You never paint the glory
    But in reflected gleams!
My pencil only pictures
    What I have known and seen:
How can I tell the joys that dwell
    Where I have never been?

I sing the songs of Zion,
    But I would never dare
To imitate the chorus,
    Like many waters, there.
I sketch the sunny landscape,
    But can I paint the sun?
Can that by art, which human heart
    Conceiveth not, be won?

The Laplander, that never
    Hath left his flowerless snows,
Might make another realize
    The fragrance of the rose:
The blind might teach his brother
    Each subtle tint to know
Of lovely lights and summer sights,
    Of shadows and of glow.

To whom all sound is silence,
　　The dumb man might impart
The spirit-winging marvels
　　Of Handel's sacred art.
But never, sister, never
　　Was told by mortal breath
What they behold, o'er whom hath rolled
　　The one dark wave of death.

Yet angel-echoes reach us,
　　Borne on from star to star,
And glimpses of our purchased home,
　　Not always faint and far.
No harp seraphic brings them,
　　No poet's glowing word,
By One alone revealed and known —
　　The Spirit of the Lord.

Have we not bent in sadness
　　Before the mercy-seat,
And longed with speechless longing
　　To kiss the Master's feet?
And though for precious ointment
　　We had but tears to bring,
We let them flow, and could not go
　　Till we had seen our King!

Then came a flash of seeing
　　How every cloud should pass,
And vision should be perfect,
　　Undimmed by darkling glass.
The glory that excelleth
　　Shone out with sudden ray,
We seemed to stand so near "the land"
　　No longer "far away."

The glisten of the white robe,
    The waving of the palm,
The ended sin and sorrow,
    The sweet eternal calm;
The holy adoration
    That perfect love shall bring,
And, face to face, in glorious grace,
    The beauty of the King!

Oh, this is more than poem,
    And more than the highest song;
A witness with our spirit,
    Though hidden, full and strong.
'Tis no new revelation
    Vouchsafed to saint or sage,
But light from God cast bright and broad
    Upon the sacred page.

Our fairest dream can never
    Outshine that holy light,
Our noblest thought can never soar
    Beyond that word of might.
Our whole anticipation,
    Our Master's best reward,
Our crown of bliss, is summed in this —
"For ever with the Lord!"

UNDER THE SURFACE

MISUNDERSTOOD

"PEOPLE do not understand me,
    Their ideas are not like mine;
All advances seem to land me
    Still outside their guarded shrine."

So you turn from simple joyance,
    Losing many a mutual good,
Weary with the chill annoyance
    So to be misunderstood.

Let me try to lift the curtain
    Hiding other hearts from view;
You complain, but are you certain
    That the fault is not with you?

In the sunny summer hours,
    Sitting in your quiet room,
Can you wonder if the flowers
    Breathe for you no sweet perfume?

True, you see them bright and pearly
    With the jewelry of morn;
But their fragrance, fresh and early,
    Is not through your window borne.

You must go to them, and stooping,
    Cull the blossoms where they live;
On your bosom gently dropping,
    All their treasure they will give.

Who would guess what fragrance lingers
    In verbena's pale green show!
Press the leaflet in your fingers,
    All its sweetness you will know.

Few the harps Aeolian, sending
    Unsought music on the wind:
Love and skill are ever blending,
    Music's full response to find.

"But my key-note," are you thinking,
    "Will not modulate to theirs"?
Seek! and subtle chords enlinking,
    Soon shall blend the differing airs.

Fairly sought, some point of contact.
    There must be with every mind;
And perchance, the closest compact
    Where we least expect to find.

Perhaps the heart you meet so coldly
    Burns with deepest lava-glow;
Wisely pierce the crust, and boldly,
    And a fervid stream shall flow.

Dialects of love are many,
    Though the language be but one;
Study all you can, or any,
    While life's precious school-hours run.

Closed the heart-door of thy brother,
    All its erasure long concealed?
One key fails, then try another,
    Soon the rusty lock shall yield.

Few have not some hidden trial,
    And could sympathize with thine;

Do not take it as denial
    That you see no outward sign.

Silence is no certain token
    That no secret grief is there;
Sorrow which is never spoken
    Is the heaviest load to bear.

Seldom can the heart be lonely
    If it seek a lonelier still,
Self-forgetting, seeking only
    Emptier cups of love to fill.

'Twill not be a fruitless labour,
    Overcome this ill with good;
Try to understand your neighbour,
    And you will be understood.

THE MINISTRY OF SONG

LIFE-CRYSTALS

THE world is full of crystals. Swift, or slow,
Or dark, or bright their varying formation;
From pure calm heights of fair untrodden snow,
To fire-wrought depths of earliest creation.
And life is full of crystals; forming still
In myriad-shaped results from good and seeming ill.

Yes! forming everywhere; in busiest street,
In noisiest throng. Oh, how it would astound us,
The strange soul-chemistry of some we meet
In slight and passing talk! For all around us,
Deep inner silence broods o'er gems to be.
Now, in three visioned hearts trace out the work with me!

A heart that wonderingly received the flow
Of marvels and of mysteries of being,
Of sympathies and tensions, joy and woe,
Each earnestly from baser substance freeing:
A great life-mixture, full, and deep, and strong:
A sudden touch, and lo! it crystallized in song.

Then forth it flashed among the souls of men
Its own prismatic radiance, brightly sealing
A several rainbow for each several ken;
The secrets of the distant stars revealing;
Reflecting many a heart's clear rays unknown,
And, freely shedding light, it analysed their own.

A heart from which all joy had ebbed away,
And grief poured in a flood of burning anguish,
Then sealed the molten glow; till, day by day,
The fires without, within, begin to languish:
Then "afterward" came coolness; all was well,
And from the broken crust a shining crystal fell.

A mourner found, and fastened on her breast
The soft-hued gem, the prized by mourners only;
With sense of treasure gained she sought her rest,
No longer wandering in the twilight lonely;
The sorrow-crystal glittering in the dark,
While faith and hope shone out to greet its starry spark.

A heart where emptiness seemed emptier made
By colourless remains of tasteless pleasure;
ONE came, and pitying the hollow shade,
Poured in His own strong love in fullest measure;
Then shadowed it with silent-falling night,
And stilled it with the solemn Presence of His might.

A little while, then found the Master there
Love-crystals sparkling in the joyous morning;
He stooped to gaze, and smiled to own them fair,
A treasured choice for His own rich adorning;
Then set them in His diadem above,
To mingle evermore with His own light and love.

THE MINISTRY OF SONG

HOW SHOULD THEY KNOW ME?

THERE are those who deem they know me well,
    And smile as I tell them "nay!"
Who think they may clearly and carelessly tell
Each living drop in my heart's deep well,
And lightly enter its inmost cell;
    But little (how little) know they!

How should they know me? My soul is a maze
    Where I wander alone, alone;
Never a footfall there was heard,
Never a mortal hand hath stirred
The silence-curtain that hangs between
Outer and inner, nor eye hath seen
    What is only and ever my own.

They have entered indeed the vestibule,
    For its gate is opened wide,
High as the roof, and I welcome all
Who will visit my warm reception-hall,
And utter a long and loving call
    To some who are yet outside.

I would lead each guest to a place of rest;
    All should be calm and bright;
Then a lulling flow of melody,
And a crystal draught of sympathy,

And odorous blossoms of kindly thought,
With golden fruit of deed, be brought
    From the chambers out of sight.

Some I would take with a cordial hand,
    And lead them round the walls,
Showing them many a storied screen,
Many a portrait, many a scene,
Deepcut carving, and outlined scroll;
Passing quickly where shadows roll,
    Slowing where sunshine falls.

They do not know and they cannot see
    That strong-hinged, low arched door,
Though I am passing in and out,
From gloom within to light without,
Or from gloom without to light within;
None can ever an entrance win,
    None! for evermore.

It is a weird and wondrous realm,
    Where I often hold my breath
At the unseen things which there I see,
At the mighty shapes which beckon to me,
At the visions of woe and ecstasy,
    At the greetings of life and death.

They rise, they pass, they melt away,
    In an ever-changing train;
I cannot hold them or tell their stay,
Or measure the time of their fleeting away;
As grim as night, and as fair as day,
    They vanish and come again.

I wander on through the strange domain,
    Marvelling ever and aye;
Marvelling how around my feet

All the opposites seem to meet;
The dark, the light, the chill, the glow,
The storm, the calm, the fire, the snow;
How can it be? I do not know;
     Then how, oh, how can they?

What am I, and how? If reply there be,
     In unsearchable chaos 'tis cast.
Though the soaring spirit of restless man
Might the boundary line of the universe scan,
And measure and map its measureless plan,
     The gift of self-knowledge were last!

THE MINISTRY OF SONG

SOME
HYMN SCORES

Another Year Is Dawning

AURELIA

Samuel S. Wesley, 1864

1. An-oth-er year is dawn-ing, Dear Fa-ther, let it be,
2. An-oth-er year of mer-cies, Of faith-ful-ness and grace;
3. An-oth-er year of serv-ice, Of wit-ness for thy love;

In work-ing or in wait-ing, An-oth-er year with thee;
An-oth-er year of glad-ness In the shin-ing of thy face;
An-oth-er year of train-ing For ho-lier work a-bove.

An-oth-er year of pro-gress, An-oth-er year of praise,
An-oth-er year of lean-ing Up-on thy lov-ing breast;
An-oth-er year is dawn-ing, Dear Fa-ther, let it be,

An-oth-er year of prov-ing Thy pres-ence all the days;
An-oth-er year of trust-ing, Of qui-et, hap-py rest.
On earth, or else in heav-en, An-oth-er year for thee.

(A Hymnal for Friends)

[203]

Golden Harps Are Sounding

HERMAS

Frances R. Havergal, 1836-1879

1. Gold-en harps are sound-ing, An-gel voic-es ring, Pearl-y gates are
2. He who came to save us, He who bled and died, Now is crowned with
3. Pray-ing for His chil-dren In that bless-ed place, Call-ing them to

o - pened, O-pened for the King! Christ, the King of glo - ry, Je - sus,
glo - ry At His Fa-ther's side: Nev - er-more to suf - fer, Nev - er -
glo - ry, Send-ing them His grace: His bright home pre-par - ing, Faith-ful

King of love, Is gone up in tri - umph To His throne a - bove.
more to die, Je-sus, King of glo - ry, Is gone up on high.
ones, for you; Je-sus ev - er liv - eth, Ev - er lov - eth too.

REFRAIN

All His work is end - ed, Joy - ful - ly we sing;

Je - sus hath as - cend - ed Glo - ry to our King!

Alternate tunes: ARMAGEDDON – 372, ST. GERTRUDE – 181
(Great Hymns of Faith)

[204]

A. S. Sullivan, 1874

Refrain

(The Hymnal of the Protestant Episcopal Church)

I Am Trusting Thee, Lord Jesus

BULLINGER Ethelbert W. Bullinger, 1837-1913

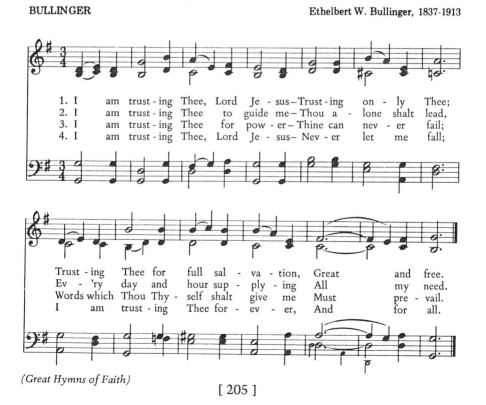

1. I am trust - ing Thee, Lord Je - sus—Trust - ing on - ly Thee;
2. I am trust - ing Thee to guide me—Thou a - lone shalt lead,
3. I am trust - ing Thee for pow - er—Thine can nev - er fail;
4. I am trust - ing Thee, Lord Je - sus— Nev - er let me fall;

Trust - ing Thee for full sal - va - tion, Great and free.
Ev - 'ry day and hour sup - ply - ing All my need.
Words which Thou Thy - self shalt give me Must pre - vail.
I am trust - ing Thee for - ev - er, And for all.

(Great Hymns of Faith)

[205]

I Could Not Do Without Thee

MAGDALENA

John Stainer, 1868

1. I could not do with - out Thee, O Sav - iour of the lost,
2. I could not do with - out Thee, I can - not stand a - lone,
3. I could not do with - out Thee, For O the way is long,
4. I could not do with - out Thee, O Je - sus, Sav-iour dear;

Whose pre-cious blood re - deemed me At such tre - men - dous cost;
I have no strength or good - ness, No wis - dom of my own;
And I am of - ten wea - ry, And sigh re - plac - es song:
E'en when my eyes are hold - en, I know that Thou art near.

Thy right - eous-ness, Thy par - don, Thy pre-cious blood, must be
But Thou, be - lov - ed Sav - iour, Art all in all to me,
How could I do with - out Thee? I do not know the way;
How drear - y and how lone - ly This change-ful life would be,

My on-ly hope and com-fort, My glo - ry and my plea.
And weak-ness will be pow - er If lean-ing hard on Thee.
Thou know-est, and Thou lead-est, And wilt not let me stray.
With - out the sweet com-mun-ion, The se - cret rest with Thee! A - men.

[206]

5 I could not do without Thee;
   No other friend can read
The spirit's strange deep longings,
   Interpreting its need;
No human heart could enter
   Each dim recess of mine,
And soothe, and hush, and calm it,
   O blessed Lord, but Thine.

6 I could not do without Thee,
   For years are fleeting fast,
And soon in solemn loneness
   The river must be passed;
But Thou wilt never leave me,
   And though the waves roll high,
I know Thou wilt be near me,
   And whisper, "It is I."   Amen.

I Gave My Life for Thee

KENOSIS

Philip P. Bliss, 1838-1876

1. I gave My life for   thee,   My pre-cious blood I   shed,
2. My Fa-ther's house of light, My glo-ry-cir-cled throne
3. I suf-fered much for thee,   More than thy tongue can tell,
4. And I have brought to thee,   Down from My home a - bove,

That thou might'st ran-somed be,   And quick-ened from the   dead;
I left, for earth-ly night,   For wan-d'rings sad and   lone;
Of bit-t'rest ag - o - ny,   To res - cue thee from hell;
Sal - va -tion full and free,   My par-don and My   love;

I gave, I gave My life for thee-What hast thou giv'n for Me?
I left, I left it all for thee-Hast thou left aught for Me?
I've borne,I've borne it all for thee-What hast thou borne for Me?
I bring, I bring rich gifts to thee-What hast thou brought to Me?

(Great Hymns of Faith)

Lord, Speak to Me

CANONBURY

Robert Schumann, 1810-1856

1. Lord, speak to me, that I may speak In
2. O lead me, Lord, that I may lead The
3. O strength - en me, that while I stand Firm
4. O teach me, Lord, that I may teach The

liv - ing ech - oes of Thy tone; As Thou hast sought, so
wan - d'ring and the wav - 'ring feet; O feed me, Lord, that
on the Rock, and strong in Thee, I may stretch out a
pre - cious things Thou dost im - part; And wing my words that

let me seek Thy err - ing chil - dren lost and lone.
I may feed The hun - g'ring ones with man - na sweet.
lov - ing hand To wres - tlers with the trou - bled sea.
they may reach The hid - den depths of man - y a heart.

(Great Hymns of Faith)

5 O give Thine own sweet rest to me,
   That I may speak with soothing power
A word in season, as from Thee,
   To weary ones in needful hour.

6 O fill me with Thy fullness, Lord,
   Until my very heart o'erflow
In kindling thought and glowing word,
   Thy love to tell, Thy praise to show.

7 O use me, Lord, use even me,
    Just as Thou wilt, and when, and where;
Until Thy blessed face I see,
    Thy rest, Thy joy, Thy glory share.
                Amen.

HOLLEY   George Hews, 1835

(The New Hymnal)

WILDERNESS   R. S. Thatcher, 1936

(The Hymnal of the Protestant Episcopal Church)

Take My Life, and Let It Be

ELLINGHAM

Nathaniel S. Godfrey, 1881

1. Take my life, and let it be Con - se - crat-ed, Lord, to thee.
2. Take my will, and make it thine; It shall be no long - er mine.
3. Take my love; my Lord, I pour At thy feet its treas - ure store.

Take my mo -ments and my days, Let them flow in cease - less praise.
Take my in - tel - lect, and use Ev - 'ry power as thou dost choose.
Take my - self, and I will be Ev - er, on - ly, all for thee.

(A Hymnal for Friends)

HOLLINGSIDE

J. B. Dykes, 1861

(The Hymnal of the Protestant Episcopal Church)

Take my life, and let it be
Consecrated, Lord, to thee;
Take my moments and my days,
Let them flow in ceaseless praise.
Take my hands, and let them move
At the impulse of thy love;
Take my feet, and let them be
Swift and beautiful for thee.

2 Take my voice, and let me sing
Always, only, for my King,
Take my intellect, and use
Every power as thou shalt choose.
Take my will, and make it thine:
It shall be no longer mine.
Take myself, and I will be
Ever, only, all for thee.   Amen.

HENDON

H. A. César Malan, 1787-1864

1. Take my life and let it be Con-se-crat-ed,
2. Take my feet and let them be Swift and beau-ti-
3. Take my lips and let them be Filled with mes-sag-
4. Take my love— my God, I pour At Thy feet its

Lord, to Thee; Take my hands and let them move At the im-pulse
ful for Thee; Take my voice and let me sing Al-ways, on-ly,
es for Thee; Take my sil - ver and my gold— Not a mite would
treas - ure store; Take my-self— and I will be Ev - er, on-ly,

of Thy love, At the im - pulse of Thy love.
for my King, Al - ways, on - ly, for my King.
I with - hold, Not a mite would I with - hold.
all for Thee, Ev - er, on - ly, all for Thee.

(Great Hymns of Faith)

Thy Life Was Given for Me

THY LIFE

George A. MacFarren, 1875

1. Thy life was given for me, Thy blood, O Lord, was shed,
2. Long years were spent for me In wea - ri - ness and woe,
3. Thy Fa-ther's home of light, Thy rain-bow-cir - cled throne,
4. And Thou hast brought to me, Down from Thy home a - bove,
5. O let my life be given, My years for Thee be spent;

That I might ran-somed be, And quick-ened from the dead;
That through e - ter - ni - ty Thy glo - ry I might know.
Were left for earth-ly night, For wan-d'rings sad and lone.
Sal - va - tion full and free, Thy par - don and Thy love.
World fet - ters all be riven, And joy with suf - f'ring blent;

Thy life was given for me: What have I given for Thee?
Long years were spent for me: Have I spent one for Thee?
Yea, all was left for me: Have I left aught for Thee?
Great gifts Thou brought-est me: What have I brought to Thee?

Last verse only:

Thou gav'st Thyself for me, I give my - self to Thee. A - men.

O Saviour, Precious Saviour

WATERMOUTH

A. H. Mann, 1889

Refrain

(The Hymnal of the Protestant Episcopal Church)

O Saviour, precious Saviour,
  Whom yet unseen we love;
O Name of might and favor
  All other names above;
    We worship thee, we bless thee,
      To thee, O Christ, we sing;
    We praise thee, and confess thee
      Our holy Lord and King.

2 O bringer of salvation,
    Who wondrously hast wrought,
Thyself the revelation
    Of love beyond our thought;   *Refrain*

3 In thee all fullness dwelleth,
    All grace and power divine;
The glory that excelleth,
    O Son of God, is thine;   *Refrain*

4 O grant the consummation
    Of this our song above,
In endless adoration
    And everlasting love;
    Then shall we praise and bless thee
      Where perfect praises ring,
    And evermore confess thee
      Our Saviour and our King.

[213]

Thou Art Coming, O My Saviour

BEVERLY

William H. Monk, 1875

1. Thou art com-ing, O my Sav-iour! Thou art com-ing, O my King!
2. Thou art com-ing, Thou art com-ing; We shall meet Thee on Thy way;
3. Thou art com-ing; at Thy ta-ble We are wit-ness-es for this;
4. Thou art com-ing, we are wait-ing With a hope that can-not fail;
5. O the joy to see Thee reign-ing, Thee, our own be-lov-ed Lord!

In Thy beau-ty all re-splen-dent, In Thy glo-ry
We shall see Thee, we shall know Thee, We shall bless Thee,
While re-mem-b'ring hearts Thou meet-est In com-mun-ion
Ask-ing not the day or ho-ur, Rest-ing on Thy
Ev-'ry tongue Thy Name con-fess-ing, Wor-ship, hon-our,

all tran-scend-ent; Well may we re-joice and sing;
we shall show Thee All our hearts could nev-er say;
clear-est, sweet-est, Earn-est of our com-ing bliss;
word of pow-er, An-chored safe with-in the veil.
glo-ry, bless-ing Brought to Thee with one ac-cord;

Com-ing; In the o-pening east Her-ald bright-ness slow-ly swells;
What an an-them that will be, Mu-sic rap-tur-ous-ly sweet,
Show-ing not Thy death a-lone, And Thy love ex-ceed-ing great,
Time ap-point-ed may be long, But the vi-sion must be sure;
Thee, our Mas-ter and our Friend, Vin-di-cat-ed and en-throned,

[214]

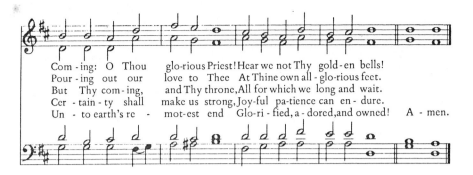

Com - ing: O Thou glo-rious Priest! Hear we not Thy gold-en bells!
Pour - ing out our love to Thee At Thine own all - glo-rious feet.
But Thy com - ing, and Thy throne, All for which we long and wait.
Cer - tain - ty shall make us strong, Joy-ful pa-tience can en - dure.
Un - to earth's re - mot-est end Glo-ri - fied, a - dored, and owned! A - men.

(The New Hymnal)

Like a River Glorious

WYE VALLEY

James Mountain, 1844-1933

1. Like a riv - er glo - rious Is God's per-fect peace, O - ver all vic
2. Hid-den in the hol - low Of His bless-ed hand, Nev - er foe can
3. Ev - 'ry joy or tri - al Fall-eth from a - bove, Traced up - on our

to - rious In its bright in - crease; Per-fect, yet it flow - eth Full-er
fol - low, Nev-er trai - tor stand; Not a surge of wor - ry, Not a
di - al By the Sun of Love; We may trust Him ful - ly All for

REFRAIN - *Stayed up-on Je - ho - vah, Hearts are*

D. S.

ev - 'ry day, Per-fect, yet it grow - eth Deep - er all the way.
shade of care, Not a blast of hur - ry Touch the spir-it there.
us to do — They who trust Him whol - ly Find Him whol-ly true.

ful - ly blest — Find-ing, as He prom - ised, Per-fect peace and rest.

(Great Hymns of Faith)

[215]

True-Hearted, Whole-Hearted

George C. Stebbins, 1846-1945

1. True - heart - ed, whole - heart - ed, faith - ful and loy - al,
2. True - heart - ed, whole - heart - ed, full - est al - le - giance
3. True - heart - ed, whole - heart - ed, Sav - ior all - glo - rious!

King of our lives, by Thy grace we will be;
Yield - ing hence - forth to our glo - ri - ous King;
Take Thy great pow - er and reign there a - lone,

Un - der the stan - dard ex - alt - ed and roy - al,
Val - iant en - deav - or and lov - ing o - be - dience,
O - ver our wills and af - fec - tions vic - to - rious,

Strong in Thy strength we will bat - tle for Thee.
Free - ly and joy - ous - ly now would we bring.
Free - ly sur - ren - dered and whol - ly Thine own.

(Great Hymns of Faith)

[216]

Peal out the watch-word! si - lence it nev - er! Song of our

spir - its, re - joic - ing and free; Peal out the watch-word!

loy - al for - ev - er, King of our lives, by Thy grace we will be.

Who Is on the Lord's Side?

ARMAGEDDON

C. Luise Reichardt, c. 1780-1826
Arr. by John Goss, 1800-1880

Who is on the Lord's side? Who will serve the King? Who will
Not for weight of glo - ry, Not for crown and palm, En - ter
Je - sus,Thou hast bought us, Not with gold or gem, But with
Fierce May be the con - flict, Strong may be the foe, But the

be His help - ers, Oth - er lives to bring? Who will leave the
we the ar - my, Raise the war-rior - psalm; But for Love that
Thine own life - blood, For Thy di - a - dem; With Thy bless - ing
King's own ar - my None can o - ver - throw; Round His stan -dard

world's side? Who will face the foe? Who is on the
claim - eth Lives for whom He died: He whom Je - sus
fill - ing Each who comes to Thee, Thou hast made us
rang - ing, Vic - t'ry is se - cure, For His truth un -

Lord's side?Who for Him will go? By Thy call of mer - cy,
nam - eth Must be on His side. By Thy love con - strain - ing,
will - ing,Thou hast made us free. By Thy grand re - demp - tion,
chang- ing Makes the tri - umph sure. Joy-ful - ly en - list - ing,

By Thy grace di - vine, We are on the Lord's side— Sav-ior,we are Thine!

.(Great Hymns of Faith)

[218]

REFERENCES

Enock, Esther E. *Frances Ridley Havergal*. London: Pickering & Inglis Ltd., 1937.

Havergal, Frances Ridley. *Life Chords*. London: James Nisbet & Company, 1880. Contains: Under His Shadow; Chords for Children; Early Poems; Miscellaneous; Loyal Responses; Closing Chords.

_____. *Threefold Praise*. London: James Nisbet & Company, circa 1892.

_____. *Life Mosaic*. London: James Nisbet & Company, circa 1893. Contains: The Ministry of Song and Under the Surface.

Havergal, Maria V.G. *Memorials of Frances Ridley Havergal by her sister*. New York: Anson D.F. Randolph and Company, circa 1880.

The Hymnal 1940 Companion, prepared by the Joint Commission on the Revision of the Hymnal of the Protestant Episcopal Church in the United States of America. New York: The Church Pension Fund, 1949.

Moyer, Elgin S. *Who Was Who in Church History*, revised edition. Chicago: The Moody Bible Institute, 1968.

Wells, Amos R. *A Treasure of Hymns*. Boston: W.A. Wilde Company, 1945.

A Hymnal for Friends prepared by the Hymnal Committee. Philadelphia: Friends General Conference, 1955.

Great Hymns of Faith, John W. Peterson ed. Grand Rapids: Zondervan Publishing House, 1968.

The Hymnal as Authorized and Approved for Use by the General Convention of the Protestant Episcopal Church. New York: The Church Pension Fund, 1916.

The New Hymnal of the Protestant Episcopal Church in the United States of America. The Church Pension Fund. New York: Seabury Press, 1940.

The New Church Hymnal prepared by a Hymnal Committee. Chicago: Lexicon Music, Inc., 1976.

INDEX OF TITLES

INDEX OF FIRST LINES